A MOMENT ON THE LIPS AT CHRISTMAS

J TAYLOR

Copyright © 2022 by J Taylor

All rights reserved. No part of this book may be used or reproduced by any means, graphic, electronic, or mechanical, including photocopying, recording, taping, or by any information storage retrieval system, without the written permission of the publisher except in the case of brief quotations embodied in critical articles and reviews.

CHARACTER LIST

Etta: A single mum. Recently lost five and a half stone. Early thirties. Works at Elm Lodge Care Home. Lives in Evie Cottage. Ex-girlfriend of Robert Ward, who is also father to Etta's daughter Chloe. Current love interest is Richie, who brings some strong Kristofer Hivju vibes.

Val: Recently divorced after her husband of thirty-one years left with no explanation. Maintains her three stone weight loss through diet and exercise. Works at Elm lodge Care Home. Has recently reconnected with an old childhood love called Adonis (yes, his real name) via Facebook but maintains they are 'just good friends'. Has two grown-up sons. Generally the voice of reason.

Nicky: Siamese cat owner/ obsessive. Lost over nine stone in under a year. Recently swapped her geeky glasses on chains and oversized jumpers for contact lenses, wrap dresses and knee-high boots. Currently in love with a much-younger man that she met online called Matt. Care assistant at Elm Lodge Care Home. Grown-up son that she rarely sees. Despite being in her early fifties, can be a little naive and far too trusting.

Jenna: Late twenties. Mother of two boys and new wife to childhood sweetheart Jason. Recently lost two and half stone for her wedding day. Care assistant at Elm Lodge Care home. Blonde, tanned and glamorous. A savage straight-talker, but always hilarious and always kind.

Yana: Moved from Russia to be with Simon her train driver husband. Slimmed down from seventeen-odd stone to just over twelve. Early forties. After a rocky start, now settled in England. Outspoken, funny and house-proud. Currently has her fingers crossed that Simon's ex-wife gets a one-way ticket to Australia for her Christmas present, failing that she'll settle for any puppy of the miniature variety.

Pam: Etta's step-nan. Likes to keep up with the Joneses. QVC-obsessed. VERY judgmental but unconditionally supportive of Etta and devoted to Chloe. Believes Lidl is vulgar. New BFFs with Jenna's mother-in-law Gillian. Wishes Charles and Diana the Corgis would put their differences aside for 'the good of the family' and produce some puppies.

Grandad: Grandfather to Etta, Great-grandfather to Chloe. Married to Pam. Eddie to his friends unless Pam is there, to which they will be corrected: 'Edward, darling, thank you!'

Gillian: Jenna's mother-in-law. Wife to Barnaby. Raging snob. Refers to her car as 'the landie'. Befriended Pam on Jenna's hen-do after the pair bonded over cosmetic surgery and a shared disgust of Nando's self-service policy and three-star hotels.

Maggie: Jenna's mum. Lover of clip-in hair extensions and copious amounts of gold jewellery. Chain smoker. VERY shouty and sweary. Considers Iceland's cocktail in a pouch a 'classy bevvy.' Heart of gold.

Jenna's nana: See Maggie and then add thirty years.

Jason: Jenna's new husband and father of Jenna's two boys. Kind-hearted.

Richie: Jenna's cousin. Broad-shouldered man mountain. Wild flame-red hair and a full beard. Ex-SBS turned fit camp owner. Etta's new love interest. Buys the most perfect awful flowers.

Robert: Etta's ex. Smary. Arrogant. Absent father to daughter Chloe. Decided he wanted Etta back because she'd lost weight. Currently having a nervous breakdown as his on/off fling has announced she is pregnant.

Porsha: Jenna's friend. Beauty therapist/ face filler technician who almost got her certificates. Gossipy. Loves a drink or ten. A bit like Marmite. Has a good heart.

Mum and Nigel: Etta's Mum and not legal stepdad due to their not legal wedding 'commitment ceremony' in Cornwall. Nigel is an anti-establishment, barefoot vegan hippy who believes Western medicine is poison. Etta and her mum have a very strained relationship.

Carly: Etta's sister. Tall, slim and blonde. Has a very important question for all of the vegans out there.

CHAPTER 1

Days before Christmas: six
Boyfriends: one (I know!)
Times I've pinched myself due to current happiness levels: 2,989,094057

Faaallaaalllaalalalaaalaaaa It's Christmasssssssssss! Well, nearly.

I suppose you are dying to know what happened after *the* kiss? Well, the morning after the wedding, thanks to Pam's business cards (as she keeps reminding me), Richie sent me a text which read:

Richie 10:42 am

Hope you have a safe journey home. Are you free for a call later this evening?

This sent me into a bit of a tiz. Call, what did he mean? Voicecall? FaceTime? After conferring with the other girls on how to respond for well over an hour, I replied:

Etta 11:58 am
Of course! X

I know that seems like a long time for a two-word reply. But there was so much to consider.

'I would just ask if he means video or voice call,' said Nicky, while pulling a concerned face. Val agreed this is what she would do too.

'No!' Yana interjected. 'Etta, do not do this. You do not ask, but you make yourself ready. Casual but the good hair, the good makeup, the nice clothes and the best lighting. Then, if he say, "Etta, shall we switch to the video?" You say "Yes, but I do not expect the video, so prepare for me not at my best." Then he thinks, who is this goddess? Is good idea, no?' said Yana, smiling broadly. 'I do this when I live in Russia and talk to Simon. He thinks I never ready, but I always ready.' Yana giggles.

'Ain't he saw her last night with no slap on, though?' Porsha points out, tearing up a second pain de chocolat from the breakfast buffet.

'Yes, but you know better than anyone, babes. There's no makeup in person and no makeup on FaceTime. I look like I've been dead ten years without concealer and two layers of foundation. Deffo don't do the video call without full make-up, mate, and Yana's right about the lighting as well. You really need to get that locked down. Nothing major, just maybe move the lamp from the lounge to your bedroom and borrow Nic's halo light. Try a few different positions and what not,' said Jenna as she zipped up her Just Married baby-pink tracksuit.

Val then said that I had to be careful as I could potentially also make a 'rod for my own back'. I hadn't really understood what she meant at the time, but nearly two weeks in now I understand completely.

The first evening we had, as Yana predicted, started on voice call. He then asked if I wanted to 'change to video'. I having spent the two hours after Chloe went to bed washing my curly hair, applying a natural-looking make-up (that takes longer than usual make-up) and choosing a casual caramel-coloured ribbed loungewear set. I had then spent a further half an hour moving around my room and positioning then re-positioning Nic's borrowed halo light until I looked less like a potato in a wig and more goddess (only slightly less, but it was something).

So I was feeling pretty smug when I casually replied 'Video? Well, I'm not really video ready, but okay if you want to.' As coyly as I could muster.

Richie had appeared on screen, lazing on his sofa in a sports top.

'Hang on, let me whack the big light on, you can probably barely see me,' he said, getting up and walking over to a light switch. I noticed Sky Sports on in the background, the television muted and a half-empty glass of water on the table.

When he plonked himself back down on his surprisingly stylish sofa, he had commented on how 'radiant' I looked. Imagine me having the neck to wave off his compliment and scoff! Yes I am a knob, but don't worry, I got my comeuppance.

As we settled into our chat, relief washed over me. I think spending time with someone in person is a good indication of how you get on, but take away the activities and the distractions and plonk two people on a phone and that's when you can really tell if you click. Our conversation flowed as easily as our laughter did. We spoke about our families, friends, what we liked to eat, hobbies and our jobs. Richie told me how busy he was with his fitness business, which was based in the Brecon Beacons.

'I really want to take you out, but I'm working right till Christmas Eve, then up with my mum for Christmas and I know you're working anyway,' he said. I had mentioned that we were all expected to put the hours in at Elm Lodge, whilst Jenna was on her honeymoon.

'How about I come down on the 27th?' he suggested. 'We could still talk every evening, would be nice to see your face. Give me something to look forward to when I'm being coaxed into a knitted jumper and force fed mince pies by my mum,' Richie had joked.

And that's when I realised what Val meant. Because now every night I would have to prepare for a video call because I have now raised my own bar. Still, it's a small price to pay as I really do enjoy speaking to him.

What other news do I have. Oh yes, you won't guess who our newest care assistant is at Elm Lodge? It's only Porsha!

After the wedding, there were some major dramas. It started when one of Porsha's clients made an official complaint about her, which led to a run in with trading standards and the local constabulary. Porsha was in a bit of a state, because even before the authorities told her she could no longer practice, she had lost most of her clients after the lady who made the complaint posted about Porsha on the St Ives Facebook page. Called her 'dangerous and incompetent' and warning others away from her services. The post got a lot of likes and re-shares. And as soon as word spread, the cancellations flooded in. That's when Porsha really started panicking because she has so many store cards, plus there's also her Brazilian bum lift that she's still paying off monthly.

Knowing that she was so upset and needed a new source of income and fast, Val agreed to put in a good word for her at work. To be fair to Porsha, we were all very dubious of how she would get on, but she's doing brilliantly so far. Especially given it's such a dramatic career change. She's even taken over the book club, but more of that later. I'm leaving to drop Chloe off now, because Val, Nicky, Yana and I are going swimming before work. We're keeping up the exercise and eating sensibly, but no more calorie counting until the new year. If you can't let yourself go a bit at Christmas, when can you?

Well, I say I'm dropping off Chloe, that's if I can wade through the Santa's grotto that is currently Pam and Grandad's front garden! You should see it. Potted Fraser firs drowning in gold baubles dotted all up the drive and around the water feature, flashing garlands along window frames and garage door, there's even a pair of twinkly reindeers and a 'ho-ho-ho'-ing santa.

Inside is the same. I couldn't even see the television in the living room after our roast on Sunday, because the four-foot-tall LED polar bear was causing too much of a glare. It's honestly like the Wayfair catalogue Lapland rolled into one.

And that's without getting into the light show outside. I did feel a bit sorry for Grandad. I mean, surely he's too old now to be up a ladder for fifteen hours in 3°C weather for three days on the trot. Admittedly, the *National Lampoons*-inspired house and roof lights are indeed 'a strong and unforgettable statement' as Pam had declared at the big switch on, as she stood drumming on her John Lewis cake tin and metal letter opener to alert as many of her neighbours as possible.

The jury's still out on exactly what the statement is, but then again, they're happy, so who cares what I or anyone else thinks?

And if my grandad chose to spend three days on his own roof, tied to the chimney for safety, whilst Pam directs him via a megaphone where she wants him to staple the next batch of five thousand lights, then I suppose that's his business. And, to be fair, Pam had sent him up there with a rucksack containing a Thermos, six rounds of ham and tomato sandwiches, two mince pies and a male portable urinal. Oh, and a waterproof jacket in case it started as the forecast indicted raining/hailing/snowing. Credit where credit's due.

CHAPTER 2

St Ives Leisure Centre, St Ives, Cambridgeshire

'Wasn't you supposed to be going there?' Val asks Nicky as we bob about in the shallow end, catching our breath as a woman wearing a sunflower swimming cap glides off past us into a rather splashy backstroke.

'I was, but then Matt's mum's oven stopped working and so Dot thought it would be easier for them to come to me,' said Nicky. *Ummm.*

'Five days early, though?' I say, holding on to the rough stone edge and leaning back, the cool of the water making my cheeks feel even more flushed. Nicky makes a few uncommitted 'umm' and 'well' noises.

'They thought it would be nice for us all to be together and get settled in,' said Nic, not very convincingly.

Val shoots both me and Yana one of her 'this is not right' looks.

'You are so laid back, Nicky. I would not be comfortable if two strangers were at the house of Yana. I will not lie, I have the big shock that you go with the flow. What about your cats?' Yana asks, pulling a face to show her disapproval and concern.

Nicky looks straight ahead for a few moments, maybe considering the points that have been raised.

'Three virtual strangers, actually. Matt's sister has also come with them. But Matt has promised to look after the cats and you know how I am. What choice did I have? Shall we do a few more?'

This is Nicky's way of saying she doesn't want to discuss it anymore. Nothing else is said on the matter until we are back in the changing rooms.

I love swimming but I hate getting ready after. The hot, damp air, the sock you drop as you're fumbling about in your bag, which lands onto the always wet tiles. I never feel ready after swimming even when I've showered and dried my hair. I used to think that it was just the local leisure centres that were like this, but Porsha's friend who works in the Marriott gym got us day passes. Gorgeous it was, the pool all lit up, a jacuzzi a steam room with eucalyptus which I spent nearly as long in as the sauna. The changing rooms were admittedly a lot nicer and you don't have to pay for the hairdryer, but it's still the same warm, damp air.

I waited for Nicky to head over the other side of the lockers to dry her hair, before gesturing for Yana to join Val and I at the sinks.

'This seems to be one thing after another with Matt, doesn't it? And Nic doesn't seem happy,' I say quietly while rubbing body lotion over my arms.

'I do not trust this man!' whispers Yana, glancing over to check Nicky is not within earshot. 'Or his family. If cooker not work why do they not call the mender man to fix it or go onto the Google and order the new cooker on next day's delivery? I do this with my washing machine. At lunchtime, I order one day and the next it comes. End of problems. I think they take our friend for the fool.'

'Should one of us go round there, maybe? Meet them and try to find out what's going on?' I ask.

'Yes, good idea. I could pop round there tomorrow after work? Make an excuse that I need to borrow something. Better than us all turning up,' said Val nodding as she wipes away stray smudges of newly applied mascara. 'Maybe the new *Pinch of Nom* cookbook. I quite fancy a read of that, actually.'

Yana said that she would like to go with Val and, to be honest, so would I, but as Val said, it would look less suspicious if we don't all turn up in force.

Jenna told Val to try and get some photos for when we update her on WhatsApp. Val said she would try. I don't think she will, though. It took her nearly two minutes to find a thumbs up icon last week.

Later the same day, Elm Lodge Care Home, St Ives, Cambridgeshire

As much as I don't agree with a lot of Anika's management choices, credit where it's due, she has surpassed herself this year with the decorations.

I know I've told you before what a handsome building Elm Lodge is, with its floor-to- ceiling bay windows, parquet floors and Georgian high ceilings; well, imagine how magical it looks with a twelve-foot real spruce tree in the entrance hall, warm white lights and red velvet ribbon wrapped around every branch. In both of the reception rooms and dining room, slightly smaller eight-foot relations also stand proud.

Gone are the old 80s threadbare tinsel and the once-shiny snowflake-fanned ceiling decorations that resembled the inside of a crisp packet. Fresh eucalyptus garlands, sprigs of fresh holly and clusters of mistletoe (which Reg has been putting to good use, especially when Porsha is on shift) have taken their place. Yana and I were taken aback when we walked in last week and saw it all.

'This look like the *Ideal Home* magazine,' said Yana, reaching out to touch the fresh garland over the hallway fireplace. 'And it is real. They spend the big bucks this year!'

Admittedly, it is all to keep up appearances with the visiting families and for next year's brochures that Anika had commissioned, to pull in new clients, but still the difference the decorations have made to the mood in the home is amazing really.

At times, morale can be a little flat around Christmas. Residents feeling rejected from living family members, who despite living close by, fail to invite them to spend the day with them or even for lunch. Previous Christmases at Elm Lodge have been a time of reflection more than celebration with many members missing ones they have loved and lost. But this year things feel a little different, Val has made sure of that.

The very same day that our manager June had announced that she was taking unpaid leave until the new year due to stress, making Val stand in manager in her absence, Val had asked us all to come up with as many new activities and treats to make this Christmas special for the residents.

'Think not just of festive activities, but ones we can all carry on with in the months ahead. Let's give them a reason to look forward to the new year. We all need something, don't we?' Val had said enthusiastically.

Val's enthusiasm rubbed us on all of staff and residents. This combined with the new decorations, have made a huge difference. Porsha has also been bringing copious amounts of laughter and joy with her each time she's on shift. Yes, she can be a little loud, but even that comes in handy here, and yes Val has had to remind her she was not supposed to smoke with the residents, but her heart is in the right place and that's all what really matters, isn't it?

This afternoon I had been giving our kitchen staff a hand by loading the dishwashers after lunch (cottage pie, roasted winter veg and jam roll poly with double cream if you were wondering) when Yana popped her head round the door.

'Etta, you have call in the office. I think it is Pamela and she say this is urgent.'

Like most mothers who get an unexpected call at work, my thoughts gallop straight to Chloe. Within seconds I have visions of her on the way to the local accident and emergency department with a broken arm, or with a high temperature. I dart past Yana, handing her the dirty plate from my hand as I pass, and charge down the corridor to the office and grab the phone.

'Hello, it's me. What's wrong?' I blurt out in a panicked rush.

'Wrong? Oh, nothing's wrong!' Relief washes over me. I can tell by Pam's singsong voice there is no emergency. 'All fine here, just calling to ask. Have you read my email, darling?' I smile to myself as I hear Modjo Lady in the background and Chloe asking 'Hey?' and my grandad replying, 'Um, that's what horses eat isn't it? Sorry, all out of hay! I do have some Blue Ribbands though?' I don't know why I was worried. Chloe is in the safest of hands. I know this because I have been Chloe. Everything they do with her they did with me. I imagine them in the kitchen, my grandad up the table reading his paper, Chloe next to her reading her *Horse and Pony* magazine.

'Well no, because I'm at work. What does it say? Yana said you told her it was urgent?' I ask, nodding and giving the thumbs up 'all okay' gesture to an anxious-looking Nicky and Yana who were hovering by the filing cabinet.

'Oh well I may have mentioned that it is rather urgent in a way. Check your inbox, darling. I sent it nearly an hour ago! I've been dying to tell you for over a week, but I said to myself: *Now, Pamela, you must be strong. You do not want to be accused of favouritism.* But I'm dying to spill the beans to you now!' says Pam, tittering to herself.

'Do you just want to tell me, then? As we're on the phone and I need to get back to work?'

'Well no, darling, because I may miss some important key points. And, like I said, I don't want to be accused of favouritism. You'll have to read the email like everyone else. To be honest, I really expected you to be checking your emails hourly, Henrietta. What if you missed something vital? With it being five days before the most important day of the year! Gosh, isn't it just magical? I can barely contain my excitement, to tell you the truth! Anyway, can you make sure you email me back as soon as you've read it, darling? I have my notifications on. That reminds me, did I mention I have the Gmail email app on my phone now? It's next to another app on my home screen, a smashing little shop called *The Amazon!* Gilly introduced me to it. It's sensational! A bit like Argos, but—'

'Okay, Pam. Will do. I really have to get back to work now, but I will get back to you. Give Chloe a kiss from me. Bye!' I say, cutting her short.

Felt a bit bad then for cutting her short. But not that bad. For two reasons, one I was at work and two because I know where the conversation was heading. Since befriending each other at Jenna's hen-do, Pam and Jenna's mother-in-law Gillian have become firm friends. Now every other sentence is, 'Then Gilly said Pammy!' or 'Oh, you won't guess what Gilly, my best friend and confidant, disclosed to me at brunch!' I'm sure I'll get my daily quota when I pick Chloe up later. Anyway the email is probably just the latest Christmas Day itinerary. Evidently my idea of urgent and important and Pam's is vastly different. I'm sure it can wait. I'll have a look at my next break.

Oh great. Now I don't want to sound ungrateful, but I just have to say this: For. Fuck. Fucking. Sake.

From: Pamela Wilson
PamelaWilsonlovesCorgis@gmail.com
To: Etta1991@icloud.com
Date: 20 Dec 2021 04:43
Subject: Very exciting news! Prompt response required!

Dear Family and Friends,

We cordially invite you to join us at Midwinter Lodge from 27 December to 1 January, in the glorious wilderness of the Scottish Highlands, for a Christmas and New Year's break to remember.

Midwinter is an extremely luxurious thatched cottage that sleeps eighteen comfortably and featured in 2020 **Your Home** *magazine. Facilities include gym, cinema, indoor heated pool, sauna, Aga and manicured grounds with fire pit. Small dogs are allowed in the house. Outdoor shoes are not.*

This break is a gift from us to you. NO financial contribution is required. RSVP WITHIN 24 HOURS as we need the final numbers for the Ocado shop. Transport via executive coach included. We look forward to hosting you! Let's make some memories!

Festive love and peace,

Pamela and Gillian

I will admit there was some initial excitement when I read it because I've never been to Scotland and the holiday home does sound very plush. Plus I had been relieved after fending off a brief thought this afternoon that Pam may had supplied the Femail editors at the *Daily Mail* the photo from Gran Canaria August 2018 (me, sunburnt and wedged into a very unflattering size 20 swimming costume. Completely unaware of the camera snapping away at me as I hunched over a plastic dining table chair shovelling mounds of cheesy chips from a tray into my mouth, while sporting more belly rolls and chins than a Shar Pei puppy.) Although pretty horrific, Pam had said it was a textbook before photo and had been trying to persuade me to allow her to send it in to everyone from *Take a Break* magazine to the George Foreman grill CEO. 'Well you did use their grills an awful lot, darling!'

So I was obviously relieved I wasn't going to be featured as the fatty to fitty of the month. (Not a real competition as far as I know, but you get the point.) In fact, I was pretty chuffed about the trip as it goes. Then I checked the email's ccs to see who else had been invited. That was when excitement evaporated and panic set in.

I still literally have no words.

In no particular order, it looks like I will be spending my festive break with: Pam; Grandad; my daughter Chloe; my sister; my mother (fuck my fucking life) and her new (not legal) toenail-chewing husband Nigel; Gillian and her husband (I can never remember his name); Jenna (thank god!) and Jason who will bring their two boys; Jenna's mum Maggie (who generally refers to Gillian as 'that c u next Tuesday' or 'that stuck-up cow'); Maggie's husband George; and Jenna's nana, who everyone calls Nana.

Oh, and I haven't even got to the best bit yet. Last but not least on the guest list is Richie – as in (to clarify) Jenna's cousin, my new-but-not-yet-official boyfriend, who I have yet to see in person since our first kiss.

That Richie.

It's not that I'm not happy at the prospect of spending time with him; it's just that we are still in that exciting, fresh, texting-every-moment-of-the-day bubble. And I really like him. I don't want him to get put off by it all being too much too soon.

Plus, as you know, we had both agreed that we'd spend Christmas with our families separately, and then go on our first proper date on 27th December, because his residential weight-loss boot camp company shuts on Christmas Eve until the New Year. But that's obviously out of the window now. I can't even use work as an excuse because Pam knows that I am scheduled to work an early shift on Christmas Eve and Boxing Day and that I have had a week booked off from the 27th December since last May.

So it's looking like our first romantic dinner and drinks date will be replaced by a ten-hour 'executive coach' journey with fourteen 'family and friends' as spectators. Followed by a five-day mini-break – again with fourteen spectators, including my mother, who never has anything nice to say about anyone, (especially me) and her unwashed husband, who is living proof that natural deodorants do not work. *Fan-fuckin'-tastic!*

You couldn't make this up.

At least I know why Pam had been so keen for me to join her and Gillian on a 'special girly shopping trip' for 'sensual but classy negligees' and '*things*'. I'm going to need a miracle for this break to not end in tears, (probably mine.) But then it is Christmas and, as they say, miracles happen at Christmas. That's why they call them Christmas miracles. Admittedly, I'm not sure who *they* are, but they definitely do say that. Plus, thinking about it, I'm probably worrying over nothing, because it is a bit late notice. I'm probably getting all stressed out over nothing. I bet most people won't even be able to come. I mean, who would even be available or willing to drop their plans for a luxury, all-expenses paid trip to the Scottish Highlands with a few days' notice? Yes, I am totally worrying over nothing. Probably will just end up being me, Chloe, Grandad, Pam, Gillian and her husband, Jason and Jenna.

Two hours later

In answer to my earlier question what people would even be available or willing to drop their plans for a luxury, all-expenses paid trip to the Scottish Highlands? It seems in fact ALL the people. Because Pam's just rang me AGAIN (thank god June isn't here or I would probably be getting a verbal warning right about now for bringing my 'home distractions to work'). Pam practically sung her update down the receiver. She's in very high spirits because everyone, including Richie – and my bloody mother – have said yes.

I don't think my 'Oh that's good news' was very convincing because Pam went quiet for a moment after then said, 'Oh don't worry, darling, I will make sure you and your young man have your own room, and you know me and your grandfather, once his head hits that pillow a bomb could go off and I've heard it all before so you can let yourself go, if that's what you're worried about.' Oh please save me.

Texted Jenna because if anyone would have anything negative to add about all this it would be her. I just received her reply and I have to say I am extremely disappointed in her.

Oh my god, this is amazing! Like totally brilliant. I've showed my mum and we are so down for this! And my nana. Mum's just spoken to her and she's going to get the bus down to Tesco to treat herself to some Bell's and a packet of Walkers shortbread to celebrate! Can't wait to see you all tomorrow, love ya!

Clearly she is drunk, or she's had too much Caribbean sun. Probably both judging by the level of enthusiasm.

CHAPTER 3

Monday 20th December, Evie Cottage, Farm Drove, Hemmingford Gray, St Ives, Cambridgeshire

My sister Carly arrived this afternoon. Chloe and I went with Grandad and Pam to collect her from the train station in Peterborough when I finished work, 'for the ride' as Grandad had suggested.

'I didn't even know she was coming,' I said as we pulled into the busy station.

'Neither did we until this morning. I gather there's been words between her and your nan,' said Pam.

This doesn't surprise me in the slightest. Between my nan's mood swings; her week-long sulks where she won't even look in your direction let alone speak to you are notorious and partly while her and my mild-mannered grandad divorced, and Carly's erratic hours and laziness, the only shock is that Carly has lived with my nan for as long as she has. But I suppose when you are unable to keep a job, and you're able to live rent-free and have your meals cooked, is quite the incentive. Plus Carly always did have a thick skin.

My grandad pulled up opposite the taxi rank located direct out the front of the station.

'Platform three, she said, do you mind going to find her, love?' Grandad asked. 'I'll try and stay here, but if I have to move I'll keep going round in a loop.'

'If we're not here, darling, wait over there by the bins,' suggested Pam. Yeah, that's about right I chuckled to myself as I made way through the station. A man in suit carrying a skateboard nearly walks into me coming out of Starbucks. I notice he looks back at me after he apologises. That's happened a few times lately. It feels weird being seen when I've been invisible for so long.

The train had already arrived by the time I located the right platform and had lugged up and down a large flight of stairs and walked across the bridge. At least I don't feel like I need an oxygen mask these days. You don't realise just how unfit you were until you get fit.

'Etttaaaa!' calls Carly as she spots me, causing several people on the platform to turn and gawp. She's wearing ankle boots, tight jeans and a clingy long-sleeved T-shirt with 'Santa, I've been a very naughty girl' across the front. She nearly drops the faux-fur caramel coat that's draped over her shoulder shopper bag as she attempts to drag along her wheelie suitcase.

'Here, I'll take it,' I say, taking the handle of the purple sparkly case.

'Thanks. God, it's so good to be back somewhere familiar. I know Bedford isn't far, but it may as well on the bloody moon! I mean, it isn't even Bedford really. Nan says Bedford, but it's a village, isn't it? Inkwell. Do you know the Co-op there ran out of Rizlas last week? Ridiculous, isn't it?' said Carly as we made our way back to the car. I had nearly forgotten how many questions she asks.

'Oh yeah, what's all this Pam tells me: you have a fella? What's he like? Pam said he was like a soldier, but for the government. Like Jason Bourne. God, does he look like Matt Damon? When can I meet him? Fuck, ain't you thin! How did you get so thin?'

That said, on the way home, Pamela asked Carly nearly as many questions as she had me.

'I thought you would be spending Christmas with your nan, darling?'

'Yeah, she was doing my complete head in. She has been on my case for weeks. Then she had a major strop last week because I wouldn't go to some cat show with her so she said she was going to spend Christmas alone this year. She's booked herself on one of those shit cruises, you know to cold places like Norway, so I thought I'd come here.'

'What about your hairdressing course, how's that going?'

'They kicked me off because I missed a few weeks when I went to Australia to watch my ex surf.'

'Oh lovely, how did you pay for that then, darling? Do you have a job now?'

'No. I can't find anything to suit me. My new boyfriend bought me the tickets and my ex gave me passes for food and drinks from backstage catering, and he let me sleep in his motor home. Bit of a squeeze because it's only for one person really.'

'That sounds fun!' said Pam, shooting my grandad a look that screamed *Did you just hear what I just heard?*

Carly suggested she come round to mine for a 'sister sleepover' when we got back to Grandad's, which took a little longer than anyone expected as Carly squealed,

'Aaawww, Burger King! Could we grab one as we are passing please, Grandad?' Which turned into Pam saying, 'Oh bugger it! It's Christmas after all, let's all have one!' So we did.

Said I couldn't do the sleepover this evening as I had plans tonight. Which was sort of a lie. I don't have plans as such, but Richie is phoning me at nine. I am cutting it fine as it is nearly half seven now and I have to get Chloe settled and be video ready by eight. And imagine if Carly was here with me. Can you imagine? Because I can; there would be me trying to keep my head to the left (my better side) while Carly my model perfect sister would be next to me leaning into the camera with both sides (she has no bad side), her indigo eyes twinkling and her mouth bursting into a Cameron Diaz smile as soon as Richie said something even remotely funny. Nah. I think I can be forgiven for giving that scenario a miss.

Richie said I looked tired tonight. That's what happens when you choose a Big Whopper and family time over an extra hour to apply a third coat of concealer and foundation. He also told me his mum Diane has now made up with Maggie (Richie's Auntie/Jenna's mum). They had a big, drunken row at Jenna's wedding, resulting in them both saying they would never speak to the other one again.

In the days after, whenever Richie asked his mum about Christmas, she had responded by saying she would be spend Christmas with Maggie and Co. over her 'dead body'. So Richie had thought he would be up in Manchester.

'So does that mean you and your mum will be at Maggie's for Christmas after all?' I asked.

Richie confirmed they would be.

'Isn't it lovely? This time of the year? It always makes people come together, doesn't it?' I gushed.

'Christmas?' asked Richie, sounding amused. 'It wasn't Christmas that got them back talking. We have *The Fall* on Netflix to thank for this latest reconciliation. My mum had no one to discuss with how if she had to be murdered by any serial killer she would love to be killed by the one in *The Fall*. That's why she backed down.' He chuckled.

'She has a good point, to be fair. Me and Nicky had a similar conversation not long ago.' He laughed then, but I wasn't joking.

Either way, this now means Richie will spend the festive period here in Cambridgeshire with his whole family.

'So I've been thinking. How about if we grab some drinks on Christmas Eve? I know you mentioned you're staying at your grandad's with Chloe. But could you spare a few hours? At least then we will have had some time to ourselves before we leave for Scotland?' asked Richie. I said yes I would love that.

So it's been decided, on Christmas Eve evening Richie will be taking me out for dinner 'and stuff'.

Five Minutes Later…

Fuck, I've been thinking. Does 'and stuff' mean sex? I bet it does because he also said 'time to ourselves'.

This makes me anxious because the thing is, I haven't done 'and stuff' since I found out I was pregnant with Chloe and she was eight a few days ago, so you do the maths. It's been a while… Like a really long while. I am feeling the pressure, because Richie I think, in fact I know, has a lot to compare me to. I wonder what his ex-girlfriends look like.

Decided I am going to ask Jenna to find them on Facebook and show me when she's home tomorrow. God, I bet they're all built like whippets with stomachs as flat as ironing boards and I'm built like a Shetland pony. I'm quickly learning that feeling good dressed in a supportive bra and well-cut clothes and feeling good naked wearing no clothes are two different things. I will have to make sure the black-out curtains are drawn. FUUUCCK. Will ask the girls at dinner this evening. Maybe 'and stuff' just means drinks, or bowling. Robert took me bowling once. He paid for it on my debit card.

Tuesday 21st December, St Ives, Cambridgeshire

Grandad arrived with Pam, just after seven, to give me a lift into town while Pam settled down with Chloe to watch a film I have seen far too many times. I honestly think I could recite the whole of *Arthur Christmas* at this point. Kids always have one film they watch over and over, don't they?

I am no one to talk though. I've seen *Dirty Dancing* so many times, I could watch it in my head. When Carly and I were kids we used have that video on a loop. We'd lay about in Grandad's lounge and argue who was going to be Penny and who was going to be Baby. We always both wanted to be Penny. 'You have to be Baby, Etta, because you have the same hair. I would always sulk because I really wanted to be Penny. Everyone wanted to be Penny. Even as young girls we had been programmed to aspire to be glamorous and blonde. How stupid we were. What I would give to be Baby now. As Pam always says, 'They don't make men like Patrick Swayze anymore.' Or, to be precise, Patrick Sqwizel as she always calls him whilst pulling a *phwoar* face. Anyway, where was I?

Oh yes, I had left to meet all the girls at The Riverview, and had pinged Val a quick text just before I got into the car to ask if she had been round to Nicky's and if she had managed to persuade her to come to dinner. Nicky has been dithering and in two minds all day today, which wasn't really like her anymore. We had all encouraged her, saying that none of us had seen Jenna since she left for her honeymoon and how it would be nice to all be together to catch up etc.

A voice note reply from Val had come through just as we hit the first set of traffic lights in town.

'Yes, I have been round there. We have also had a very frank chat, so she's coming and has something to discuss with us all over dinner. See you shortly.'

The pub is heaving, not unusual for this time of the year. Although it seems to be mainly work dos having sit-down meals. I am glad Yana booked our table.

'Oh my god, you're like so tanned, babes!' squeals Porsha as an even-more-bronzed-than-usual-looking Jenna saunters through the crowd towards our table. Our high-spirited waves are short lived as Jenna spins round whilst holding out her ring hand like a puppy with a sore paw and bellowing, 'Whoop whoop, Mrs Henderson in da house!' Only to lose her balance and fall dramatically sideways, only being saved by a sparse-looking Christmas tree.

The estate agents, who I recognise from passing the Thomas Morris windows most days, are seated next to us all cheer and whoop as Jenna takes a bow and blows a kiss in their direction. We are still howling with laughter as she saunters over to us like nothing has happened.

'Fuck me, I nearly stacked it then!' Jenna giggles, stating the obvious as she drops her Michael Kors bag on the floor and slides into the booth next to Yana. 'Married life is making me a lightweight, I've only had two mugs of wine with my mum and Nana before I came out, just to beat off the jet lag. So anyway, shall we order before you all fill me in on what I've missed? I'm starving!'

We all decide on fish, chips and peas. 'It's basically Christmas, after all,' says Porsha. With our food order in and a fresh round of drinks in our hands, we start to bring each other up to speed.

'Right, I have some news, so I'll start,' says Val, sipping her brandy. 'Adonis and I have had a little change of plan. When we got onto the topic of Christmas on the phone the other evening and I mentioned that we had snow forecasted next week, he told me how much he missed Christmas feeling like Christmas, with the weather in Greece being so mild and whatnot. So on the spur of the moment we both decided that instead of me visiting him, he will join me here until the new year…' Val pauses as our food arrives. Why do we all do that when someone comes over to your table? We could be talking about the weather, but we would still all stop dead, as if we were midway through a classified discussion of top-secret information that is strictly need-to-know only.

We take it in turns to smile awkwardly and muttering 'thanks so much' or in Jenna and Porsha's case 'cheers, babes'. Yana even starts stacking empty soda glasses into each other to accommodate her plate of food which she was then warned was 'extremely hot'. As soon as the waitress excuses herself with a 'enjoy your meal', Val continues.

'And then I will be taking a month off to fly back with him and see how things go.' From Val's uncharacteristic lack of eye contact I know she is feeling embarrassed, although I am not sure why.

After the year she's had, I say good on her to be honest. We all need to grab the happy moments with both hands.

'That's fantastic news, mate, but will you get the time off? You know what June is like. The trouble I had to get my wedding and honeymoon covered!' asks Jenna, wiping off the tartare sauce that's found its way down the front of her black-roll neck jumper dress.

'Well, that's where I come in, babes,' Porsha announces. 'As you all know, I'm unable to do my usual job at the mo due to, well you know, and so I've started at Elm Lodge. 'So today I have been given all Val's shifts from January 4th, and any other shifts that they are short on!'

Since Jenna's hen-do, Porsha had been joining in on our group chat. Which was when we encouraged her to apply for the relief hours position at work.

'Did you hear any more from the police since the arrest?' asks Yana. 'I still do not believe they come to the house of your mother and put you in the handcuffs!'

'Yeah they're leavin' it to Trading Standards now, babes. After they nicked me and kept me sweatin', the rozza in charge decided that I ain't actually committed an offence, cos there ain't no law about injectables. But Trading Standards has said it's probably better I don't do it no more; well at least till the woman's solicitors have finished suing me. Thank fuck for insurance!' said Porsha, raising her Red Bull and vodka. We all follow her lead and raise our own drinks, that meet in the middle with a clink, while swapping bemused side glances.

'I also have some news, but before I get into that is everything okay, Nic? Val mentioned she called in to yours?' I ask. Nicky finishes her mouthful of food, picks up her paper napkin and wipes her mouth.

'Well I don't know really. I wasn't going to mention it, you know how I am, it is probably just me being a worry wort but Val said I needed to. As you all know, I was supposed to be going to Matt's mums for Christmas. I had even ordered the cats some new carriers, but then they kind of invited themselves to mine instead. Because of their broken cooker.' I notice Yana and Jenna swapping 'I don't believe that at all' looks. Val nods in Nicky's direction. There's obviously more to tell.

'It's just that since they arrived a few days ago, they have kind of taken over a little bit. And well, I'm not sure if it's because of his mum and sister being there, but Matt and I have also yet to, you know, *do the deed*.'

Porsha squints and pulls a perplexed look of confusion making it clear that she in fact doesn't know at all. Jenna stands up and helpfully gestures a thrusting motion with her arms at Porsha, nearly knocking over my drink in the process. Still, it seems to do the trick.

'Ohhh *that* deed!' Porsha laughs as she drains her Smirnoff Ice.

'That isn't all though, Nic, is it? Tell them what you're really worried about.' We all look at Nic, who is pushing the remains of her battered haddock around her plate.

Val sighs. 'Shall I tell them?'

Nicky nods.

'What Nic is actually worried about is that her guests may have actually moved themselves in!'

'What do you mean, moved themselves in? Why do you think that, Nic?' I ask as my hand races to guard my wine glass from another of Porsha's very generous refills.

'Well, as Val said, me and the cats had been invited to Matt's mum's for Christmas, but then Matt texted me and said that their oven had broken and so his mum suggested they came to me instead. I agreed thinking it would be just for the day or maybe Christmas Eve through to Boxing Day, and the next thing I know they was on my doorstep.'

I can tell by the way Nicky has rushed through her explanation that she is not happy with the current situation and that there is a lot more to it.

'So why you think mother of Matt and Matt move into house of Nicky and not just here for the celebrations?' asks Yana.

Val shoots Nicky another exasperated *just tell them* look.

'Mainly because they arrived with quite a lot of personal possessions,' Nicky replied quietly. Jenna who has now had quite a lot more than a 'few mugs of wine' tries to reassure Nic.

'I got hit with a fifty-six quid excess baggage for my honeymoon, mate, so maybe they are like me and just don't travel light.'

Val sighs again as she waves to an acquaintance she's spotted heading towards the toilets. Her face returns from all smiles to serious as they pass.

'No, this isn't over-packing. I've seen it for myself. There is an old van that they arrived in, stuffed to the brim with everything you could imagine, which is, as we speak, parked on Nicky's driveway.'

'What kind of things are in the van?' I asked.

'Literally everything you'd imagine. I saw a vacuum, a deckchair and a slow cooker, just through peeking through the windscreen when I had a nose,' said Val.

Over the next hour we discuss every possible reason for Matt and his family arriving in a van filled with seemingly all their worldly goods.

'Maybe they borrowed the van from a friend and all the shit in it belongs to them,' Jenna offers, but none of us are convinced. Various other explanations into the mix for consideration; maybe Matt lied about his job and is a house clearance man, or they are hoarders to the extreme. In the end, it's Porsha that comes up with the most likely scenario.

'To be honest, babes,' Porsha says, patting Nic's hand. 'I think they are probably homeless and were never really goin' to have you at their gaff cos they ain't got one and they was always going to invite themselves to yours to get their feet under the table, and if you don't make it crystal clear that they ain't welcome after Christmas, they will probably still be there for the next one.'

Panic is now etched all over Nicky's face. Yana gives her a hug while we all reassure her that we will help her get to the bottom of it.

'The way I see it, they are never going to answer your questions honestly, so we need to do two things,' says Val, sliding back into the booth after stepping outside for a cigarette with Porsha and Jenna. 'One, find out their previous address and everything else we can about them, because let's not forget that you met him on a dating site. What do you really know about him? I mean facts and not just what he's told you?'

When Jenna mentions the Tinder Swindler, and asks Nicky if she has met his friends, or seen his debit cards when he's paid for things, Nicky starts crying and admits that she hasn't ever seen a document or a bank card with Matt's name on and no one has offered to pay for groceries and the transfer he claimed he sent to pay for half of the hotel stay at Jenna's wedding never came through.

'Exactly, babes, he's clearly full or shit, so we need to check he is who he says he is,' Porsha says.

'And two, and this is very important, you need to clarify that come Boxing Day evening you expect them to be gone,' said Val.

I half expect Nicky to defend Matt, but she doesn't. Not a word. This, given how she has previously jumped in when anyone of us have raised concerns previously, is a worry in itself. Nicky knows something isn't right.

'Do not panic, Nic, we will help you with this. Maybe we all think bad things for no reason. Maybe they do not try to live in house of Nicky. I mean I think in my heart they do these things, but we must find out the facts,' says Yana.

'Yeah, babes, knowledge is power,' says Jenna, leaning over Porsha's plate to swipe a now-cold onion ring.

It's initially proposed that Nicky should try to find out their address in Lincolnshire, 'if they even have one' as Porsha again points out. Jenna says Nicky should also sneak a look at Matt's bank card. Nic starts crying again then and says she is worried about skulking around in case she gets caught.

'I don't know if I have it in me,' admits Nicky feebly.

'Honestly, don't stress, babes, if you give it a go and bottle it or just can't get the goods, it's no bother I'll pop round with some of my uncle's sleeping pills,' reassures Porsha. 'We can just crush them and whack it in their drinks. Out for at least six hours they will be. Then we can check their pockets and go through everything in their van and phone.'

Everyone chuckles at this, apart from Jenna, because she knows Porsha isn't actually joking.

'We can't drug them, mate,' says Jenna, 'but Porsha does have a good point. What if Nic gets them out of the way? We could have a look through their stuff for clues.'

We all agree it's a good idea. I am fully expecting Nic to launch into protests.

'Do you think you could get them out of the house tomorrow after work; take them to Nando's or somink?' Porsha asks.

'Better make it Frankie and Benny's, mate,' interjects Jenna. 'Nando's will have you served and out within the hour.' Nic considers all this for a moment.

'I think let's just wait to see if they leave on Boxing Day. I will pluck up the courage and make it clear they need to return home by then. Maybe say my son is visiting. I could be clinging to the wrong end of the stick,' Nic said.

'Whatever you want, Nic, mate. We will help however you need us to,' says Jenna. I can tell she's frustrated. So am I.

I excuse myself, saying I am just going to the toilet. Yana and Val rise to their feet. 'I'll join you,' says Val, brushing down her plum blouse.

'Me too. Even though the toilets are not good for my mental health; too much talc and suckie-in knicker flashbacks!' Yana said, picking up her bag.

We make our way through the heaving crowds of diners in paper cracker hats towards the hallway to the toilets.

I ask Val what she made of Matt's family and how the situation seemed to her.

'The mother, Dot if I remember rightly. All smiles. The sister said nothing, didn't even glance in my direction. Both were just glued in front of the TV. There was something else that was a little strange, now I think about it again. When I said to Nicky, should we take our drinks into the other lounge, she shook her head and said, "Okay, but I think the duvets and cushions may still be out. Give me a moment to make some space." Matt must have been ear wigging, because he appeared out of nowhere and said, "Sorry, I haven't had time to pack my sleeping bag away yet." And hurried in there, collecting up a hold-all and a pink canvas shopper.'

'What he is sleeping in the sitting room?' I asked. 'Why isn't he in Nic's room? He stayed in her room at the wedding.'

'That is very, very strange. And also, what he do all of the day? How he have no time to tidy up?' Yana agrees, shaking her head.

'It is strange. And do you know what is even stranger? There were clearly two sets of people's belongings and two sets of pillows and duvets. Which means…' asks Val, already knowing the answer.

'That more than one person has been sleeping in the living room of Nicky!' says Yana.

'Surely Nicky hasn't given up her room?' I said, frowning.

Val admits she didn't want to ask Nicky, but as Nicky had just told us, her and Matt had not yet been together 'romantically' as of yet.

'I hope they leave the house of Nicky and do not come back,' said Yana.

'I didn't ask who the other sleeping bag was, so I could be completely wrong, but it does looks like Nicky has given up her room, doesn't it?' replied Val, holding open the door as Yana and I pass through. 'I mean, what other explanation is there? One room converted to an office, one room is Nicky's and one spare. It has two double beds though, that's what I can't work out. Surely the mum and daughter would share?'

'So why the two sleeping bags?' I ask. 'None of it makes sense.'

CHAPTER 4

Wednesday 22nd December, Evie Cottage, Farm Drove, Hemming Gray, St Ives, Cambridgeshire

All day today Jenna kept saying things like: 'You're gonna love your pressie from Richie!' And: 'I can't wait to see ya face when you open your present from Richie!' Which is either Jenna being sarcastic because it's a really shit present, or it's a really brilliant present; either scenario is completely plausible, and both scenarios would mean that Jenna really couldn't wait to see my face. Men aren't very good at presents as a rule, are they? Not that I am one to talk about crap presents. I am usually amongst the other stressed and very stupid shoppers on Christmas Eve clutching Olay bath sets and pacing the aisles of Boots, mobiles glued to their ears, muttering things like, 'Well what about a foot spa with massage jets? No? Well some bath bombs, then? FUUCCKK, well, what about a new hairdryer?' Swapping 'I'm in the shit' nods, all feeling the pressure bearing down on us like a ten-tonne brick. This year I am a changed woman. No, I haven't turned into one of those smug organised people. It's all thanks to Pam (who's probably sick of receiving a 3 for 2 bath set and a gift card) taking me aside and urging me to 'get ahead of the storm'.

It was on one Sunday afternoon in early October. The remnant of the beef roast lunch had been cleared away: 'Waitrose meat counter, 19.90 a kilogram, but you get what you pay for darling!' Grandad, who had been given 'the look' coaxed Chloe away from the television 'to find something to do'.

'Now, I need you to sit down because I have something important to show you, darling,' Pam had said as I had been summoned to join her on the new DFS corner sofa, that had been delivered a few days previously. I think I still have PTSD from having spent the best part of six hours in the show room with Pamela back in July, whilst she had repeatedly examined every part of each sofa, and asked so many questions about the two frontrunners, Florence in Cappuccino Cream and Camilla in Beige Biscuit (in case you were wondering) that the shark-like sales team who usually as good as cling to your ankles started to bury their heads in their clipboards and dart towards the glass box office to hide whenever Pam power-walked towards them calling, 'Young man, *excuse me*, young man! I need to converse with somebody in management regarding the possibility of commissioning bespoke cushion zips!'

Pam had settled on a three and two-seater with a foot rest, insisting they marked it up as 'Poofeeey' on the receipt. When I had admitted that I'd preferred the Camilla as we made our way home, Pam had pursed her lips and sighed.

'Me too, darling, if the truth be known, but one has to stick by a moral code. I wouldn't be able to hold my head up high in the street if I had a new three-piece suite named after *that woman*. I am still getting over how I was spoken to after I suggest them re-naming it. *Out of the question* indeed. They will be losing a star on Trustpilot for that, don't you worry!'

So there I was, sitting on the new sofa, as Pam thrust a laminated article from a *Take a Break* magazine in my direction.

When I had asked why she still had a January *Take A Break* magazine in October, and why it was laminated, she'd 'ha-ha'd' and said, 'I saved it for you. And you know I don't get half as many opportunities to use the laminator as one would have hoped. Now, full disclosure, Henrietta. This is going to be a difficult read, darling. But it's also a very important one and I am here to support you all the way.'

The headline was *FAMILY CHRISTMAS RUINED BY ARGOS.* The story focused on a dinner lady from Bedford called Cindy who, in order to save money, had left her present shopping until the last moment to take advantage of the sales that start on Christmas Eve, which sounded sensible enough.

However, the article divulged that not only did Cindy not end up saving any money, but she also, in fact, completely ruined Christmas for herself and her whole family, including her son called Levi (aged eleven).

Levi, the article explained, had taken it particularly badly. This was due to him having had a traumatic year at school, which had resulted in him been unfairly permanently excluded a few weeks before due to his undiagnosed ADHD making him throw a chair at his teacher's head.

On the second page Cindy was quoted saying that she couldn't get her Levi a certain Nerf gun he had his heart set on, or even another duplicate model, nor the universal television remote that her husband had been dreaming of, because both items were out of stock in the 'poxy' Argos store which was a short walk from their housing estate.

The article went on to mention that Argos had stock of both items in their next town, but that it wasn't an option for Cindy or her partner to travel the six-mile round trip to another Argos branch in order to avoid ruining Christmas, due to them both being unable to drive as they had been at the pub since opening and had indulged in 'quite a few more than a few pints'.

'It was Christmas Eve you see, mate, so we'd had some jars at the local, like every normal person on Christmas Eve! And at the end of the day, why should we have to travel? Argos is at fault, not us. They should have had stock!' ranted Colin.

Pam took one look at my wide-eyed, amused expression and misjudged it for panic.

'I know it is a hard-hitting read, but it's also a valuable lesson, darling. It could happen to us. Even Marks and Spencer's runs out of things at Christmas.'

I nodded, trying to swallow down the laugh clawing at my throat.

'You need to take this seriously. If not for yourself, then for your grandfather, Chloe, and me,' Pam had then informed me, as she shook her head while staring at a photo of the very miserable-looking couple and their little boy.

The photo also had some kind of grey filter to make the rather scruffy-looking Argos look ever more dire. The husband, Colin, was holding out an old Bush TV remote held together with brown tape, while Cindy stood the other side of Colin grimacing and giving the thumbs down gesture with one hand. Her son, Levi, could just about be seen to the other side of her, and seemed to be throwing deuces at the store, although I can't say for sure due to the magazine blurring out his hand.

Below the photo was a quotation: 'Our Levi is proper traumatised, he spent the whole of crimbo crying his eyes out, he didn't even eat his dinner. The poor sod had been looking forward to his Aunt Bessie's roast spuds and Turkey Twizzlers all year. We are thinking of suing, cause like what kind of shop runs out of stuff on Christmas Eve? It's a f******g disgrace!' Colin, 39 Very powerful stuff.

When I joked that they were all dressed like members of the Blazin Squad in their matching Fila tracksuits and Ellesse trainers, Pam had tutted and replied, 'Everyone deserves a good Christmas, Henrietta. Even the ones who go to public houses and wear sportswear on the day before the most important day of the year.'

So I had relented, made lists, and dipped into my savings (that I've since replenished with overtime shifts) to purchase and wrap all of my presents by the beginning of November. Apart from Richie's, of course, because I didn't even know him then, not properly anyway. I have played it safe and got him the new Ollie Ollerton hardback and some Dior Sauvage aftershave, which I know he wears. Pam's got him a tray of toffee from her and Grandad. When I said I wasn't sure if Richie was even a lover of toffee, Pam had looked at me like I was completely mental and said, 'It comes with its own little hammer, darling, what's not to love?' Which was a fair point, I suppose.

I wanted to mention the Richie stuff to Jenna when we spoke earlier, but it would be a bit weird for her, I think, with him being her cousin. So I am going to ask Yana at work and see what she suggests. I'm quite looking forward to work actually. It's Porsha's book club's next meeting this afternoon.

I have to say, it's a raving success so far. Especially since last month's, run by June, was a near World War Three situation. Val had been the one to come up with the idea for a book club during one of the staff meetings. June, who is always keen to impress the owners, took the idea as her own and ran with it nearly as fast as she then regretted it. I never knew so many people could have such strong opinions over a Sophie Kinsella. I thought it was going to get physical at one stage. I had to take Mary off for a slice of lemon cake to calm her down. Reg had started the heated discussions, slamming the book down on the tea table, declaring it a 'complete waste of f'ing time! Complete rubbish! And not one bit of smut!' June had tried to pass the club back over to Val then, who refused to 'out of principle'.

When I asked Porsha how she had ended up with the role, she said, 'I don't know. I said reading was my hobby during my interview, cos that's what it said to say on the internet, then Jan—'

'June,' I correct her with a little laugh.

'Yeah, her, babes. She's all like: "Oh fab, well, I have a special job for you!" And I'm like: "Oh alright then." And so yeah, that's how it all came about really,' Porsha said, flicking her hair.

I was a bit concerned when Nicky had then asked Porsha what genres she liked and Porsha had replied, 'Erm well, *Heat* magazine and *Daily mail* showbiz bar mainly, babes. But I also read Katie Price's *Being Jordan*, which was so inspirational.'

Despite our initial worries, Porsha wasn't at all fazed, and, after taking the time to listen to the feedback from the existing members, and exchanging a few texts with Maggie, whose 'read shitloads of proper books', Porsha announced that she had carefully selected a book 'to give the people what they want'.

Jilly Cooper's *Riders* was the chosen title for her first club. June seemed a little put out in her weekly 'keep me in the loop email' that almost twenty residents had signed up to this month's club, twelve more than her month. Porsha then sent round a sign-up form (bit of paper from the office and a pink fluffy pen from her pocket) declaring that she had been assured that her choice had 'Loadsa sex for you, Reg'! and a right sort called Rupert Campbell-Black for all you, ladies. Absolute sex god!' Not even Margaret could resist this sales pitch, and she signed her name muttering that she 'may as well' as there was 'little else to do'.

Porsha had come up with another good idea when she had sent the sign-up forms round, which seemed to get a lot more people on board.

'So if you are signing up, write your name on the form. And if you want to join in but are blind or whatever, don't worry! because there are audiobooks also available. That is a book that someone reads out loud and records it on a tape so you can play it back,' Porsha had explained. 'No one misses out on my watch.' She giggled warmly. 'I will be listening to the audiobook myself and you're all welcome to join me.

'Won't it be cosy?' Porsha had asked the room. 'We can grab some chairs and cosy blankets, and have a bit of wine and some choccies?' This had certainly got the chatter going, with even residents who read regularly signing up to listen to the group audio sessions. So I'm really looking forward to hearing everyone's thoughts today.

It was in the staff room that I decided now was the time, despite Jenna being there, to ask Porsha for advice. I was getting more than a bit desperate, having already asked for Yana's advice earlier. Yana had sucked her lips and admitted she wasn't the best person to ask due to 'things in the bedroom of Yana and husband of Yana are not very not good. We are how you say stuck in the missionary rut.'

'I need some advice, Porsha,' I announced as I stir my Cupasoup.

Jenna looks momentarily put out.

'You know I'm going out with Richie on Christmas Eve, well, he said it would be for dinner 'and stuff'. But it has been so long since I've *done stuff*, I am nervous. I mean, do people even *do stuff* so soon? And I don't even know if I know how to *do stuff* anymore!'

'I am going to vom up my pasta if you don't stop saying *stuff*, mate,' Jenna says, grimacing.

Porsha nods confidently and drains her cup of tea. 'You're in safe hands, babes. I will give you some tips to seduce him. And you don't forget how to shag, mate, but I will tell you what I told Val when she asked me.' Val kept that conversation quiet, I think.

'All you need to do is watch, and you need to write this down, babes,' says Porsha, gesturing at my phone. *365 days* on Netflix. All the tricks you need right there. That goes for you Yana, mate, as well, that will give you some right good tips to spice things up and to get you to get back on the saddle, Etta, or should I say dick.'

I don't even have to look at Jenna to know she is disgusted. Porsha remains completely oblivious and carries on.

'My new boyfriend is that obsessed with me after I tried out some new moves I learned after watching the new one, cos there's like three of them now. Series, I mean. So I got him really going like, in the car that much that he begged me until we did it again in Tesco cafe toilets on Saturday. We only went in for a fry up! Standing up against the changing table in the mother and baby changing room we was! You should get Richie to do this move, right, what he did was when he lifted my—' Jenna, who no doubt has a very unwanted visual of her cousin mid-lift of my god only knows what, interjects, 'It's already gone one, mate, what time is book club?'

'I've told my members half one, babes, I better ram this in quick,' Porsha says, gesturing to her ham sandwich. 'I ain't even got the chairs set up in a circle yet. Anyway, all you lot need to do is get yourselves on Netflix.'

We are all going to watch it together tonight round mine. Even Val sheepishly said that she'd join us to watch it again, after admitting it was 'certainly informative'. Nicky also agreed that she would come, as she would like to be prepared for 'when the moment comes for her and Matt'.

'She is burying her head in the sand,' Jenna said. 'We can't let this go on much longer.' We all agreed, but also agreed with Val that we have to respect Nic's wishes 'unless it gets to the point that we have no choice but to step in'. The question is, what do we deem the situation 'at the point' because, from where I am standing, we're are not far off it now.

'Well, this new book is a bit more like it!' said Reg as he takes a seat next to his friend, Henry. Even Margaret had said that the latest listen/instalment of

Riders was 'most enjoyable' when Nicky had asked her for feedback.

This was our the first discussion meeting. And the turnout was so good that we had to fetch some more packs of Jammie Dodgers from the kitchen stash.

'Loved it!' declared Joanie. 'Helen reminded me a bit of myself, actually.'

'I actually thought Helen's description reminded me of you, Margaret, in the photos on your bookshelf, when you was young,' I said, because it really had.

'I thought the same! What did you think, Margaret?' asked Val, giving me a wink.

'I am inclined to agree,' nodded Margaret, trying to hide the smile forming on her thin, red-lined lips.

'I wish I was, Helen, imagine meeting a man like Rupert,' said Joanie. All the women, us staff included and new resident James, whose husband was a jazz singer, sighed and agreed.

'I don't mind Rupe either, to be honest with you. I mean I don't swing that way, not that I have any problem with it, mind, but I can see the appeal. If I was a bird, I mean. Reminds me a bit of myself as it goes,' said Reg in complete seriousness. 'Now, who's for bringing these listening sessions to twice a week? I'm going to be honest with you all. I just don't think I can wait a week to know how Helen gets on visiting Rupert at the show. It's bloody gripping, ain't it?' asked Reg. This was met with a loud chorus of 'hear hear'. And, just like that, Rupert Cambell-Black fever at Elm Lodge Care Home was sparked.

Having just Googled how long a woman should wait to have sex with a new partner while walking home, it seems if you want them to respect you, you must make them wait for at least six dates. I have decided I will definitely be making Richie wait, because I obviously want lots of respect, but then I thought that I maybe just need to wait until after one date, as he is very respectful already and we have done a lot of FaceTime. I mean six dates is just a guide, isn't it? It's probably a bit like starting a baby on solids; open to interpretation, everywhere says six months, but I know loads of mums (well not *know* as such, but read their posts on Netmums) that were spooning baby rice in their infants mouths at four months because they 'just knew' they was ready. Have also decided to do a deep clean, change the sheets, put fresh flowers on the bedside tables and prepare the open fire in my room, just in case. As Pam says; fail to prepare, prepare to fail.

Later the same evening

Well, if Richie is expecting me to do the acrobatics I have just watched, he's in for a major let-down. I can barely sit cross-legged, let alone some of the eye-watering moves I've just witnessed on what can only be described as borderline porn. Porsha made it clear after that we was to 'adapt it to our abilities'.

'Fucking hell! The only part of Anna I think I can replicate is to copy her personality and act well stroppy and moody and that,' Jenna said. She then scrunched up her face and poked her tongue out at me when I said that Jason probably wouldn't even notice a difference.

When Yana asked Val how the tips from the film are working out for her and Adonis, Val groaned and said, 'Well a bit too well, actually.' This got our interest.

'Have you put his back out trying to copy the boat scene?' Porsha asked. 'That's what happened when my fella tried it. Still using Ibuleve gel now he is. Left it in my mum's bathroom the other day and she ended up brushing her teeth with it. Got it mixed up with Colgate!' She cackled.

'Much worse than that, we had a little bit of an upset yesterday. I can't believe I'm telling you this,' said Val, rolling her eyes to the ceiling. 'We had decided to watch a film in bed, taking with us the nice bottle of red we had treated ourselves to, with the Sainsburys shop.'

'So much for just good friends!' chuckles Jenna.

Val smirks and raises her eyes to the ceiling again. 'After finishing it, without going into too many details, one thing lead to another.'

'As these things tend to do,' said Yana, nodding.

'Exactly as these things do,' agreed Val, a wry smile forming. 'So one thing led to another, and, as bad luck would have it, we were getting right to the end of *things* and, well, it was fairly vocal.' Jenna nudges me with her elbow and I can feel her shaking holding in her laughter. I daren't look at her as I know she will set me off. 'I did think that I heard a knock on the door, but ignored it thinking it was maybe the Avon lady or suchlike. In hindsight, it was past eleven, but I wasn't thinking straight at the time.

'Mind was on the job,' said a nodding Porsha without a hint of humour. Me and Jenna burst into laughter.

'Yes thanks, you two. I'd save the giggles for later. There's more to come.'

Which just made Jenna belly laugh even more. Val who's also laughing now as she says, 'It's really not funny.' Before carrying on her story. 'About thirty seconds later, we've forgotten all about the knock we thought we heard and things are really coming to the end. Imagine my utter horror when, all of a sudden, we hear men's voices in the hall. Adonis looks at me and I look at him. There's no mistaking that there's people in the bungalow, but before we can fully stop what we're up to, there's a bang bang on my bedroom door.'

'Oh my god!' I say, gasping and trying not to laugh.

'Yes, oh my god indeed. I didn't know what to think, because before I even had a chance to make myself decent I heard my son's voice calling through my now-open door: "Mum, can you come into the lounge, please? The police are here with me and they need to speak to you."'

'The Old Bill? What they were doing in your house? How did they even get in?' Jenna asked as her eyes bulged with intrigue.

'Both my sons have a key for emergencies. Never in a million years had I thought they would ever use them. Unless it was an actual emergency, of course. But Richard clearly has a different idea of the term emergency than I do. So where was I. Oh yes, naked in bed with Adonis and my son asking me to come and speak to the police. I somehow managed to pull on some clothes and made my way down the hall with the shred of dignity I had left to face not only my son, but what turned out to be two male policemen. Both of which, it was clear from their lack of eye contact, had heard and knew exactly what I had been up to just minutes before.

'"Terribly sorry to bother you. We were called to 13 Craven Street this evening after reports of a domestic disturbance. It became clear on attendance that although no offence had been committed, your son Richard was both heavily intoxicated and unwelcome at the address."

'"The address that I fucking own," Richard had muttered. The younger policeman reminded Richard to remain calm while the older one carried on explaining the situation to me.

'"We decided, rather than to take him into custody to sober him up, we would ask him if he had anywhere else he could go and sleep it off and, well, he said here with you. So we are sorry to disturb your, erm, evening, but we just needed to check that he was able to stay with you. Can you confirm that it is okay with you?"'

'Before I could even open my mouth, Andrew turned to me and said, "The cow has chucked me out, Mum! It was only one kiss and few texts. She's being unreasonable! Well sod her cos I don't want to go back now anyway. I will live here with you! Keep you company. At least you know how to iron a shirt!"

'While we waved off the police from the doorstep, Richard only turned to me and said, "What on earth did you have on the telly earlier? We could all hear it from outside! It sounded proper raunchy! From those coppers' faces, I think for a second they thought it was coming from your actual bedroom. Imagine that at your age!"

'Then, in film-perfect timing, Adonis appeared at the top of the stairs wearing my peach silk dressing gown. I am sure you can all imagine Richard's face. I honestly do not know which one of us was more mortified!'

'He think you were watching film like the *365* and then he sees Adonis and he knows what the police know already; that you was doing the fuckie fuckie!' Yana says, wiping away the tears of laughter streaming down her cheeks.

When we finally stop crying, I ask Nicky how things have been with Matt and his family staying at hers since we last spoke.

'Well, you know, it can be a little awkward at times. Only because I don't know them very well yet. But Matt's sister did make a nice meal yesterday evening. And I told them my son was arriving the day after Boxing Day, and they said that was fine.'

'Let's hope they got the hint then,' Jenna said, looking as unconvinced as the rest of us.

CHAPTER 5

Thursday 23rd December

Found Pamela playing Rod Stewart's 'Roxanne' on repeat and staring at a packet of Maltesers this afternoon when I called in after work to collect Chloe. Usually Now Christmas 2002 only plays in the month of December under that roof, so I knew immediately that something was wrong.

'You okay?' I asked Pam.

'To tell you the truth, darling, no. No, I'm not okay. You give give give and this was the final straw. I feel like cancelling the whole thing. Pack away the tree, the lot,' she replied dramatically.

I ask her if it is to do with the trip and some of us taking over an hour to reply to the opt in or out activity list.

'No, darling, it's to do with this!' she says while grasping the box of Maltesers. 'I've seen some low blows in my time, but this, this just is too far and I won't have it!'

I make Pamela a cup of tea and ask her who's upset her. 'Gosh, I am shaking with rage and shock, I just can't believe it,' Pam said before telling me the whole 'disgusting and mortifying' story.

The story started on Monday when Pam had popped round to her friend and neighbour, Sally, to deliver her presents. 'A double-layer box of Thorntons, wrapped in John Lewis holly paper, with matching tag and bow,' said Pam who paused, clearly waiting for my reaction.

'How lovely of you,' I said with as much enthusiasm as I could muster.

'I know, darling, that paper was two pounds per sheet. That's per sheet, not per roll,' she added to clarify.

'Very nice,' I add as she tutted.

'And so I take it round to Sally *in the rain* because your grandfather was helping Bert fix something to other. So there I am, standing on her doorstep with my new Land Rover brolly which my lovely Gilly, my actual friend that appreciates me, gifted me for being me. Anyway, where was I? Oh, so I say, "Here you go, Sally, darling, Merry Christmas. And she's all, "Oh, Pamela, I don't have yours ready yet. I will call round with it tomorrow." So I think, *Okay, exceedingly rude to not invite me in or offer me a lift home*.'

I cough to disguise my laugh here because you can see Sally's house from Grandad and Pam's driveway. Pam offers me a water.

'No, you carry on, what did the selfish madam say?' I ask.

'Oh no, not this again, Pamela,' my grandad says, coming into the dining room to retrieve a pen.

'If it was your friend that had gaslighted you, you would have plenty to say! Let me have my voice, Edward please, this is my experience and I will not be silenced.' Someone has been reading too many Harry and Meghan biographies.

'I give her the benefit of the doubt, but then she doesn't call around as promised on Tuesday or Wednesday. And I know it isn't just because she hasn't been out, because when I was walking Charles and Diana, I saw Arnold, you know Arnold from the bungalow round the other end, who used to own the cake shop down by the chip shop?'

Know it? I have probably eaten everything on the menu a thousand times over, I think, my mind wandering. I wonder if they still do those delicious pink ring doughnuts.

'So I say, "Oh, can't stop, Arnold, as I don't want to miss Sally," and then he says, "I saw Sally in the doctor's yesterday." So obviously by then I'm reeling. And so you can imagine how I feel today when her husband knocks on the door and hands me these!' She's shaking the box of Maltesers now. "These are from Sal," he says. "Merry Christmas!" Not even wrapped. I wouldn't mind, but those chocolates were continentals. The disrespect is absolutely disgusting.'

'I would have cancelled it already if I hadn't already had paid for the turkey. But I still might. She's pushed me over the edge. Maltesers indeed!'

I spent the next hour encouraging Pam 'not to let the cow get to you!' And for her to 'think of Chloe and me' before cancelling Christmas and also reminding her that we had our 'special ladies night this evening!'.

'You're right, darling,' Pam said eventually. 'She won't bring me down. To think I nearly cancelled the Waitrose made-to-order Yule log. Next year she will be getting a Christmas card from the same box I give to the postman and the family on the end of the road that don't mow their lawn. She will wish she had never crossed me.'

'Out of the box?' I ask her.

'Yes, darling, you know, the really cheap, revolting ones you usually buy. The ones you pick up in Tesco in packs of ten.'

So there you have it. If you ever get a Christmas card that looks like it's come 'out of the box' from Pam you know you have pushed her too far.

Decided to ring Porsha before bed to ask her about waxing, after all the 'bring back the bush' talk at work today, thanks to the book club's latest instalment. Not the sort of thing I wanted to ask in front of all the others.

When I asked her where I should go and what I should ask for, she replied, 'Well you have two choices, babes. All off or a Brazilian, you know, like a landing strip. To be honest, you've left it well late, you're off ya head if you think you'll get a booking this late. It's Christmas Eve tomorrow, babes!' Like I had forgotten. 'Don't stress though, I can do it. I still have my gear.'

I was a bit reluctant because of, well obvious reasons, but as Porsha said, she's 'waxed loads of minges' and never been arrested. So she's coming round after work tomorrow. Sure all will be fine.

CHAPTER 6

Ladies Night, St Ives Rugby Club, St Ives, Cambridgeshire

I had wondered when Pam and Gillian accepted Maggie's invitation to attend a ladies' night at the local rugby club if they fully understood what such nights usually entailed.

I can confirm after witnessing them sharing the stage (and a bit more in Gillian's case) with 'Father Cockmas' and his 'Horny Helpers' that they definitely didn't, but they definitely do now.

Gillian had arrived at Pam and Grandad's and held out her car keys in my grandad's direction with a request for him to park 'the Landie' in the garage for 'insurance purposes' before helping herself to a single grape from the fruit bowl in the kitchen.

'Are these the Duchy Organics we picked up in Waitrose, Pammy?' she enquired while delicately biting minuscule pieces. 'They are delicious.'

'They are, Gilly, and I agree, they can't be beaten, Although I expect nothing less from His Highness, such a clever man,' said Pamela as though Charles had personally grown and picked the bunch of sable grapes especially for her.

Thankfully, the riveting conversation was cut short by our taxi, signalling its arrival with several toots.

I was looking forward to seeing everyone, but I am embarrassed to admit I was feeling a bit put out that Carly had tagged along, swooping in and taking Jenna's sister Clemmie's ticket, after Clemmie's boyfriend had surprised her with a holiday to Goa. Not even going to lie, it was the childish scenario of they are my friends and I don't want you playing with them. I mean at this stage Pam probably sends more texts each day to Jenna than she does me, but well, it's Pam, isn't it? It's different.

The venue was very village hall prior to lottery funding, but it felt festive with George Michael's 'Last Christmas' booming out and copious amounts of white felt stapled around the stage. Baubles and fairy lights had been Sellotaped to the ceiling with duct tape. I agreed with Nicky that the place had a 'rustic charm'.

'What wines do you have, please?' Pam asked a barman who had some strong George Best vibes about him, (drinking era).

'Red white,' he replied briskly while tipping a pile of greasy-looking cocktail sausages from a baking tray into a large chipped bowl on the bar.

'White menu, please,' said Gillian, as Pam narrowed her eyes at the bowl which unless I'm mistaken and Carlsberg also makes serving dishes, started its life as an ashtray.

'House red, house white, that's the menu, love,' the now-smirking barman replied through hoarse chuckles. Gillian huffed and sighed like a martyr, finally settling on a Rémy Martin 'in an *extremely* clean glass'.

'Alright, mate. Mum was just telling everyone how great St Lucia was. Glad I'm home though, missed my mates, didn't I?' Jenna says, grinning as we join the rest of our group at the table. Even Porsha who had stayed late at work, and had to get changed in the staff toilets had made it.

'It's true, ballin' her eyes out she was on one night at the hotel disco,' said Maggie, handing out a tray of drinks at random. 'It was the song that set her off. Spice Girls' "Goodbye", weren't it, Jen?'

Jenna nods solemnly.

'It was,' said Jenna, giving us the doe eyes. 'I heard that and thought I miss you lot cos you are all my spice girls,' said Jenna. The last line does it for Val, who chokes on her rum while belly laughing.

'That's one I haven't been called before,' says Val through hoots as Pam passes her a hankie out of her evening bag.

'Sobbin', she was,' said Maggie. 'Enrico from the bar come over with another jug of cocktails, didn't he, bless him? He thought she was ballin' cos he had just refused to serve us anymore booze, didn't he, Jen?'

Jenna nods her head in agreement. 'He did, yeah. It was after you almost fell in the pizza oven, weren't it?' said Jenna, nodding to us all.

'Nah, mate, that wasn't that night, the night we are talking about was the night when Jase had got confused about the water fountain.' He thought it was a urinal, bless him,' Maggie explains to the group. 'I said, now I'm not being funny, but if you start putting a load of fountains round a family pool, us English we ain't used to it, you're going to get the odd confusion.'

Yana looks confused. 'What is fountain?' she asks.

'Exactly, mate. See, it's not just the English,' says Maggie.

I was about to ask which Spice Girl Jenna allocated to me (I had my fingers crossed for Posh) when Gillian rose to her feet while saying 'good grief' under her breath.

'I need to use the facilities, would you like to join me, Pammy?' said Gillian, picking up her Chanel handbag, her coral nails holding onto the strap on her bony shoulder as though she is about to walk through a notorious gang-run housing estate late at night.

'Grab us another round, Gill, mate! The show should start soon, just tell Charlie behind the bar to do another Russian roulette for twenty! Like Quality Street then, ain't it? A nice surprise that way! Oh, and a tray of shots! That will keep us going till the boys arrive!' bellowed Maggie. Neither Pam nor Gillian responded. They didn't need to. Their faces said it all.

I will say one thing for alcohol; it's an excellent social leveller. Gillian and Pam had initially turned their noses up at the drink equivalent of a lucky dip, but later relented on the next round, ditching the cognac in favour of 'Maggie's mindblower' sloe gin fizz (actually made with Beefeater, not sloe gin and Schweppes lemonade instead of fresh lemon juice, due to bar stock availability). I'm not really a gin drinker, but when you are with Jenna and her family there is a lot of encouragement to be an anything drinker. Carly, unsurprisingly, fitted right in.

While Nicky is discussing pet food brands with Yana, who is hoping to get a dog after Christmas, I listen to Porsha, who's filling in Pam and Carly, the only two people who hadn't already heard her blow-by-blow account of her arrest.

'I tell ya, the mo-shon-nal torment I have been through. And the damaged eyelash extensions!' raged Porsha, trying and failing to put her mouth around the straw in her glass.

Nicky asked what happened to Porsha's eyelashes. 'I was bawling my eyes out for two days solid I was, on account of me thinking I was about to get sent to Holloway and become Big Bertha's new plaything. Fucked them right up it did. They're not meant to get wet. The way I was treated; no telly, no WiFi, no phone! I've rung up a no-win lawyer, they're goin' to sue the lot of them.'

'Too right!' said Carly, accepting another glass of unknown alcohol from Maggie. 'It's discrimination, that's what it is! Against the beautiful! I get it all the time!' Carly slurred at Porsha.

'I still do not believe they come to the house of mother of Porsha and put you in the handcuffs!' tuts Yana.

'Absolute liberty. I can't believe it either!' agreed Carly, shaking her head, her hoop earrings glistening in the disco lights.

The rest of us swap bemused side glances, because after seeing the before and after photos that the accuser posted on Instagram, we can believe it.

'Gosh, how exciting! I wonder what the show will be,' shouted Pam, clearly not taking Genuine's 'Pony' being played on repeat as a sign of things to come. By the time Cambridgeshire's answer to Peter Andre's dad appears in a pound shop Santa outfit, and has slid across the stage on his knees (possibly part of the show, possibly occupational hazard of being eighty per cent body oil) and grabbed hold of his bulging crutch with one hand, and bellowed who wanted to see what he had in his 'massive sack' into the microphone in the other, Pamela had sidled up to me and said in a low voice, 'I don't want to worry you, but I have a feeling he may be a stripper, darling.' No shit, Sherlock.

To be fair to Gillian and Pam, they joined in with the clapping between drinks, despite their obvious distaste. And Gillian only told Maggie to stop flashing her boobs a few times, then gave up and let her just get on with it.

Gillian had resisted slightly when she was selected by the horny helpers to join Father Cockmas on stage to discover if she was 'norty or nice', but then relented and said she would 'come quietly' as long as they 'made it quick' and 'respected her space'.

Maggie had grumbled that she had told that 'c u next Tuesday' how much she wanted a 'proper going-over' from the big man in red herself, while she and Gillian had been downing their tequila and that Gillian had therefore only gone up there 'out of sheer fuckin spite'.

'She won't even get the full benefit of the experience, prudish old cow. She should have given it to someone like me who would. I mean, she washes her hands after touching raw meat, no way will she be up for half of what I would be. Selfish cow.'

I can however report Maggie was wrong. Gillian couldn't have had more of a full experience if she tried.

After the four horny helpers, who all looked a bit Boyzone the reunion, had seated Gillian on a plastic chair on the middle of the stage, they wasted no time in turning their attentions to various members of the audience.

Father Cockmas reappeared, now armed with a '30 per cent extra free' Iceland squirty cream, and by the time he was a minute into his (quite enthusiastic) routine to 'Mr Bombastic', Gillian, whose whole face had reached a shade of vermillion, had been grinded on and squirted at and more times then I heard Jenna say 'I can't fuckin wait to get these photos on Facebook!'

When Mr Cockmas was down to only his G-string, Gillian's last shot must have kicked in, and having gained some vodka-based bravery, she was doing as directed and whipping Mr Cockmas with an oversized candy cane as he straddled her suggestively.

It was all good clean fun until the crowd's chants of 'off off off' as a garage version of Pretty Ricky's 'Grind With Me' prompted one of the horny helpers to tug off the Velcro G-string just as Mr Cockmas was unfortunately in mid groin pump, while straddling in close proximity to Gillian's face, who had been, even more unfortunately, in mid gasp at the time.

'Mother-in-law of Jenna was tonight talking to me about the Christmas lunch she will prepare, but I now think she no need to cook. She eat her meat and two veg early this year, on that stage!' says Yana, throwing her head back in laughter.

'That should have been me,' muttered a bitterly disappointed Maggie.

'Oh my god, my eyes. There are some things you cannot unsee!' Jenna said, standing on her chair to allow her phone's camera zoom to work at its best.

We were all still roaring with laughter when Gillian had skipped back to the table, accepted the vodka Val had offered her as an 'antiseptic' and sat grinning like a Cheshire Cat.

'I love you lot. I might move back in my grandad's now, just so you can all be my mates!' said Carly as we staggered outside to wait for our taxis. 'Especially you, Gillian! You're my idol!'

I don't know if it was Carly's declaration or the blast of frosty air that sobered Gillian up a bit as we stood outside waiting for our taxis.

'It was the vodka. I have been drink spiked!' Gillian declared. Pamela agreed, tapping her friend's arm and offering her a sugar-free polo.

'Accepting drinks and downing erm ain't actually called spiking, Gill, mate. You are just a binge drinker now like the rest of us. Get over yourself, mate,' declared Maggie.

Gillian made us all promise we'd 'never speak of this evening again!' as the two Ford Galaxy taxis pulled into the car park.

'So now I tell you my plan,' says Yana, turning round in the passenger seat.

Val and Nicky look at each other. I know they think that Yana is talking about something to do with Nic's guests, but I know they're aren't. Because Jenna and I have seen what Yana had in her bag this evening.

'I already tell you all that the sex with the husband of Yana is very boring. Before it very good, but now it is same and very boring,' said Yana, unfazed by the taxi driver next to her currently making an O shape with his lips. 'So when I read the book of Porsha's book club, I think I wish Simon is Rupert. Because Rupert is the rude but also very sexy man. So tonight before I go home, I take my bag and put on this…' Yana passes her phone in the back. I take the phone and look first as Val and Jenna peer over my shoulder.

'Bloody hell!' giggles Jenna, throwing her hand to her mouth. The photo is a selfie of Yana in the rugby club toilets. She's posing in the mirror in a sheer white blouse, her foot – in shiny riding boots – is on the sink, her legs covered in cream breeches and a riding crop in her hand.

'Blimey!' Nicky says, putting on her glasses.

'This is photo I send to Simon,' confirms Yana.

'Simon, he wait for me on the hale bale in lounge which we make look like stable with kitchen table on side as door. When I get home Simon will be wearing the crash riding hat on top of the blond man wig and jodhpurs. Tonight he is not Simon, he is the Rupert and I am the Helen.'

I have no words.

'Where did you get the hay from, mate?' asks Jenna through cackles.

'Simon go to the riding centre of Etta and Pam and say he buy hay for his goat.'

There is a few seconds where no one says anything as we are too busy wheezing with laughter. Finally Nicky composes herself and says, 'Hay can be very dirty, I hope Simon thought to put a rug down, your poor carpets. Imagine the stains.'

'It's not the hay stains I would be worried about, mate, to be honest!' says Jenna, shrieking.

CHAPTER 7

Christmas Eve, St Ives, Cambridgeshire

Chloe stayed round at Grandad and Pam's last night, so I popped in before work to have some breakfast with them all. Found my grandad crouched down in the dark at the end of his drive, shoving a ten-pound note into a washed-out Dolmio jar.

'What on earth are you doing?' I ask.

'Shhhh' replies Grandad. 'I don't want the neighbours to hear.'

I ask him if he has started a dead drop drug empire, but he claims he is not the Walter White of St Ives and is in fact 'just bribing the binman'.

'They are so militant with these bins! I miss bin bags. You could have put a hundred of them out here before all this recycling nonsense! I just can't get rid of the rubbish, there's just too much of it.' He gestures to an admittedly staggeringly impressive pile of boxes in every size and shape you could imagine. They all have the telltale Amazon black tape.

'I don't know who told her about Amazon bloody Prime, but I have a few words for whoever did. I don't stand a bloody chance now. At least with that QVC it took three to five days to arrive. I just can't keep up with it now.' Grandad's still shaking his head as he leans down and picks up a rectangle box that's almost as tall as me.

'Guess what came in this?' he asked, waving it about in a slightly manic fashion.

'Umm, an ironing board?' I venture.

'You'd think so, wouldn't you? But no, it was a pair of socks and a lip balm! Honestly, the world has gone mad! I think there's someone at that Amazon shop out to wind me up!'

Grandad lowers his voice now as he speaks, barely moving his lips, 'I've spoken to Marek, the head bin man, and we have come to an agreement. He will take whatever I put out here, even garden waste, every time they come, and I will pay him a tenner a week.'

'Couldn't he lose his job for that?' I ask.

'Not if he don't get caught he won't, so don't tell anyone, especially—' He gestures his head towards Pam, who is wearing a knitted jumper with a Scottish dog on the front in a Christmas hat, making her down the drive with another bag of rubbish.

'Hello, darling! Happy Christmas Eve. Wasn't last night fun! Chloe and I have just been setting up the new place settings ready for the big day! So I thought I would pop out and add this to the pile,' she says, gesturing to the stack of empty John Lewis cracker boxes. 'Our refuse collector is absolutely second to none, darling. The lovely man takes everything your grandad leaves him. I've told my ladies in club the other day, I said, "Now, ladies, if you have any excess recycling or general rubbish, do not worry, my bin person takes everything! So pop it around to mine the day before collection, it's not a problem at all! Some collectors can be so finicky about amounts and colours and what not; we're so lucky that ours takes anything! That goes for you too, darling, any excess rubbish, let us know and we can leave it out here with ours. Just tell your grandfather and he will come and collect it in the trailer, won't you, darling?"'

'Thanks, Pamela,' I say, smirking at my grandad, who has the expression of someone who knows he will soon be paying a lot more than ten pounds a week to get rid of not only his own rubbish and his Amazon-addicted wife, but also that of everyone she knows.

'Ohh, Amazon van!' Pam sings as a van pulls up next to us and starts unloading. 'That must be the walkie-talkies and the paper shredder! How exciting!'

Carly comes downstairs as I'm finishing my egg on toast. 'Pam, can I have some paracetamol and a can of coke, please?' asks Carly.

Pamela scrunches up her nose. 'Painkillers, yes, tooth-rotting drinks? Not before lunch, darling,' Pam replies, handing her a glass and gesturing to the jug of fresh orange juice on the table.

'Grandad said we are all off out with the girls again later, and your fella will be there. I can't wait to meet him!' Carly said to me, leaning over Chloe to reach a sliced of fried bread from of grandad's leftovers. The grease oozes over her fingers as she takes a large bite.

'You don't mind me tagging along, do you? Mum and Nigel will be here soon and I know Mum will bring up Cornwall again. God, she's so bloody dramatic. I mean, I ask one question and she acts like it was the main event of her wedding.'

'I'm only going for a few drinks until I meet Richie at six. He is taking on me on a date kind of thing,' I say.

Pam tries to bail me out. 'I thought you'd want to stay here with us and make sausage rolls and watch a film with Chloe, your grandfather and I, Carly?' Pam gives Carly the *yes you do* look. If Carly picks up on it, she does a good job of pretending she doesn't.

'Nah thanks, Pam. I'd rather go for drinks with Etta and say hello to her fella. Make sure he's good enough for her.' Oh great. I nod.

'Come round mine when I finish work then,' I say as Pam tuts and shakes her head. *Why can I never just say no?*

Yana, despite us all asking repeatedly how last night went, had said only, 'I tell you after the work.'

My shift today was so much fun. Each one of us staff members had brought in a selection of food and drinks and laid it out into the television room for the residents to enjoy whilst they settled down and watched 'White Christmas'. I thought my eyes were deceiving me when I saw Reg making suggestive innuendos to Margaret via a chocolate finger.

'Did you just see that?' I asked Porsha, narrowing my eyes in astonishment.

'I did, babes, yeah. Great, ain't it? They're like all in love now and shit. Book club brings people together, don't it?'

When I asked Reg later about his new, budding relationship, he replied, 'We are seeing how things go. But seems like a perfect match, don't it? Me Rupert's double and Marg who's still a ringer for Helen. We ain't putting a label on it. I don't want to be tied down,' said Reg, shaking on his cardigan. 'I have a lot of offers as it goes.' We both laugh then.

'How's your love life? Jenna told me all about you and her cousin,' said Reg. Of course she did.

'Good, I think, but I haven't been in a relationship for a long time and we are quite different. He is into keeping fit.'

'Yeah, Jenna said he was Special Boat Service. Well, you know the saying opposites attract, ay? Look and me and Marg. I used to think she was a right stuck-up old mare, which she is in a way, but there's more to her than that. You can get too used to being alone if you're not careful, my love,' Reg says. I am just thinking he seems very out of character when he calls me back, 'Oh, Etta, love, before I forget, Morrisons has Baileys three quid fifty off. You couldn't grab me a bottle, could you?' Ah no, all fine there, I think, grinning and nodding my head in response.

A lot of people moan about this time of the year, but I love it. Like, adore it. It's the cosiness of it. Not just Christmas Eve, but the late autumn and winter months in general. The afternoons like this one, where it's not quite dark, but the skies are muted charcoal and the crisp, icy air stings your throat if you breathe in too deeply. We have been going to the small cafe next to the river a lot recently. It's owned by a man that we met at yoga. A bit on the trendy side, with bare brick walls and tables made from chunky reclaimed timber. But despite the on-trend decor, we are always welcomed warmly and the prices are more than reasonable.

The six of us settle down by what has fast become our table. Circular with stools tucked into an alcove by the front window, I really like this spot. The river is peaceful while the footpath is always busy enough to provide a healthy dose of people watching.

'Ooohh, dear,' said Val as we witness a little boy of maybe three or four with the most awe-inspiring curly chestnut hair tripping over as he passes the window.

'Bless his heart. It will be those shoes. Boys and laces don't mix. Max was forever falling over in his last school ones, we went with Velcro this term.' Says Jenna.

'Least he's okay,' says Val. 'That could have been nasty.' We all agree as we watch the adult with the boy rush to pick him up and dust off his palms.

'Come on then, Yana, don't keep us in suspense. Do you need to lend my nana's Vax for that carpet of yours or what?' said Jenna, sipping her skinny latte, smirking.

Yana sighs.

'Okay. Now I tell. So you know the ex-wife of Simon and son of Simon and the wife of son of Simon and that they come today, Christmas Eve, to spend Christmas at house of Yana?' Yana asks, biting into a gingerbread man that has a white iced beard and red coat.

'Very festive,' Val says, nodding as Yana gestures to the biscuit.

'I do not very like ginger, but I buy because it reminds me of Gillian and father of the cock,' Yana adds, which makes me almost choke on my drink.

'I think you are very brave to blend the families,' said Nicky, getting the conversation back on track.

'Well this is what we thought too,' Yana agrees. ' So where I was? Yes, so last night I go home. I go in and say, "I am Helen and wish to speak to Rupert Campbell-Black about him giving me the ring of marriage." So Simon say, "Okay I am the Rupert Campbell-Black, you, Helen, come sit on the hay bale and tell me why I give you the job of my wife when I very sexy man who can have any wife I want." So I, Helen, say, "Well I very good at the job of wife. I cook, clean and look after the house of Rupert." Then I also say I am "very excellent at the riding". So then Simon, who is being the Rupert Campbell-Black, say, "You is very good rider? Well, Helen, I think I be the judge of this!" So I show Rupert I am the good rider!'

The last part breaks us all into roaring laughter. A woman eating a cheese roll had swung around then and raised her over-tweezed eyebrows at Jenna, who had been biting her knuckle and wheezing pretty much since Yana had begun.

'Sorry, Yana, do carry on,' said Val, wiping away her tears.

'Is no problem, if I was you I would laugh too,' Yana says, picking up her story.

'So I am giving the riding demonstration and Rupert say, "Yes, you can ride, this is true. But do you know how to discipline? As this is very important when you will be dealing with a stallion." And so I pick up the riding crop and say, "You, Rupert, is stallion! Now you get on all fours for the discipline!" So he does and I smack him on bottom. So this is all very good. Then we get the knock at the door.'

'See, happens to the best of us,' I say to Val, who pulls her *very funny* face.

So Simon be Simon now, not sexy Rupert, and say he best see who at the door, so he go to see, but I think he forget he still dressed like Rupert, in the blonde wig and crash helmet and tight horse-riding trousers. I think maybe is Amazon. So no problem. Then, because I drink all that mystery drinks mother of Jenna give me, I think it is funny to shout, you know for the laugh, "Mr

Campbell-Black. You are best rider in all zee land, come, you must back so I can ride again and again!" When I say that this I do not know who at the door, but then after I say this I hear voices shout, "Surprise." Then I know.' Yana pauses again now so we can get our laughter under control again. My stomach is actually cramping from all the deep belly howling.

'Who were the voices?' asks Nicky, blowing her nose.

'The voices are son of Simon, ex-wife of Simon and wife of son of Simon.

I hear Simon say, "Oh, we not expect you today." And then they say, "Yes, because we do the surprise." Then Simon say, "Oh, well we now wrap your presents, so you not come in and instead you must go to shop and then come back soon." Then Simon son say, "Dad, why you dress like rider of the horses?" So Simon reply, "Because I much love the horses now. So I do the riding." And then ex-wife of Simon ask, "What you wear the wig and helmet for?" And Simon say, "For the joke." Then no one say anything until Simon say, "Okay, see you in one hour then, bye." And he shut the door.'

I honestly thought we would wet ourselves or get asked to leave the cafe. Or both. We have never laughed so much, and we have laughed a lot.

'It's all their own fault. People need to stop calling round unexpected,' said Val.

'Do you think they knew what was going on?' asked Jenna, still laughing.

'Well the son of Simon, he believes Simon love the horses. I know because today at the breakfast he say, "Yana, may I have the quiet word, please." Then he say,

"Where my dad go to the lessons of horse riding please? I will pay for more lessons for his Christmas present." But ex-wife of Simon, I think she not believe because she reads the book of Jilly Cooper, *Riders*. I know this because when she come back, she says to me, "I am more of a Billy woman myself."'

I asked Nicky and Val if they definitely can't come out for a little while this evening, and suggested that they could bring their partners with them.

'Richard is out with his friends tonight so Adonis and I are going to make the most of it, or I would do,' said Val. Nicky said that she would have liked to have come, but that Matt had texted her and said he was too tired and wanted to stay home and play his Xbox. I urge Nic to come without him, she says she 'will see'.

I had felt a bit of mum guilt for going out on Christmas Eve, but as Pam pointed out, 'You're usually working on Christmas Eve anyway, and you've had no life whatsoever for the last I don't know how long, so go and enjoy! Chloe and I have a very full schedule anyway.' I asked Chloe if she would rather I stayed and she had looked at me blankly and shook her head.

Richie had rung me while I was waiting for Carly to decide between two near-identical hanky-sized dresses.

'I've just got here, are you okay?' Richie asked me. Just hearing his voice made my stomach flip.

'Yes, I'm good. Did you get my text about my sister?' I asked.

'I did yeah, no bother. Me and Jase will head in town soon and then meet up with you all when you're ready, then we can go back to yours if you want or just stay out.' Oh my god, he wants to come back to mine.

Decided to mention this to Pam, because I always stay with her and Grandad over Christmas.

'Pam, I've just spoken to Richie and he mentioned that he might stay at mine tonight as Maggie's is a bit overcrowded,' I venture, stretching the truth.

'Good idea, darling! As long as you're here first thing, that's fine with me,' Pam replied, giving me a knowing wink. Oh god.

I was still thinking about what may or may not happen later and waiting for my sister who despite having had all day to choose something to wear had only just selected an outfit and was now standing in her dressing gown while Pam ironed it, when Porsha had called and said that her, Jenna and Yana had been home and were now waiting outside my cottage.

'Val sent this round for us!' said Porsha, holding up a large bottle of Ouzo by way of greeting us when we finally arrived at mine.

'Oh yummy!' said Carly. The only person I know to have ever called Ouzo yummy. 'Are we having a pamper night? I thought we was going out?' Carly continues, spotting Porsha's beauty supplies stacked by the front door.

'Nah, babes, this is to get Etta ready for her hot date.'

Jenna and Carly wasted no time cracking open the Ouzo while Porsha set up. I had said we would have to set up the 'waxing station' as Porsha kept calling it, in the lounge because my bedroom was a no-go due it being 'a right mess'. But it was really because I had it all set up for the rampant sex session that definitely will not be happening later.

Half hour later, the curtains are drawn and Porsha has made it clear that only herself, the 'beauty pro-fess-shon-al', is allowed past the kitchen door, 'for my client's modesty'.

I can hear Jenna urging Yana to re-tell her role-play anecdote to an already hooting Carly, as Porsha turns to me and says, 'Right-o, babes, get ya drawers off! Let the dog see the rabbit!' I can't say I am particularly comfortable, but, as Porsha always tells us, she's seen it all before. Plus, let's be honest, any woman that's had children is long past self-modesty. Half of the NHS had a good gawp *down there* when I was in labour with Chloe. So I think of Richie and his reaction later when he sees I am not only a domestic goddess who has all the moves (Thanks to Netflix and *365.*), but that I also look the part too. That makes me think, *just go for it*.

'Bloody hell, babes, have you been on one of those bloody bring back the bush protests or what?' Thank god you didn't get it on with Richie like this! The poor sod wouldn't have found the wood from the trees down here!' Porsha cackles. 'You're in safe hands now. Let's go for a Hollywood, shall we?' I nodded, not remembering what that actually entailed. Still, it sounded glamorous enough.

'Yep, let's go with that!' I enthused.

Porsha laid out a little wooden lolly-like stick and a mountain of beige fabric strips next to her now-bubbling wax pot.

'Bloody hell, Carly, don't mind me!' I screeched as my sister barged into the room just as I felt the warm, gooey wax make contact with my, well, you know what.

'Oh don't be such a dick! We used to share the same bathwater. I've only come to pump up the tunes!' Carly said, reaching for the remote and raising the volume to MTV Base.

'Right, brace yourself, babes. This might sting a bit,' Porsha told me as she pressed the strip down on top of the section of wax, took hold of the end and ripped it off.

'WHAT THE ACTUAL FUCK!' I screamed while Yana, Jenna and Carly sniggered the other side of the door.

'Cor, I felt that!' Jenna called in, laughing.

'I was expecting it to hurt, but that was ridiculous. On a scale of one to pushing out a nine pound baby, it was very close to the baby,' I whimpered in complete seriousness. Still, at least it's all over with,' I said. 'Thanks, Porsha, appreciate it,' I said, gathering up the towel round my waist and swinging my legs off the portable bed.

'The silly cow thinks she's done!' calls Porsha to the others. Imagine my horror when Porsha explains that she's 'removed a tree, but there's still a whole woodland to go'. I call to Carly to bring me some of the Ouzo that Val sent round.

'You just told me off for coming in there!' said Carly.

'For god's sake, stop messing about and bring it in quickly,' I directed as Porsha reached for another fabric strip.

The next thirty minutes pretty much went as follows; wax strip on, shot of Ouzo, wax strip off, lots of swearing from me, closely followed by lots of laughing from Jenna, Yana and Carly, Porsha directing me into yet another position, not to dissimilar to what I had seen on *365* on Netflix, more wax on, and so forth.

It got better the more I settled into it. I think my pain tolerance increased. Or maybe it was, as Jenna had suggested, more due to my 'booze levels'. Either way, it was nearly over and I was feeling pretty good.

'I'm just going to ask Yana and Jenna for advice,' Porsha said, heading off into the kitchen and closing the door behind her.

This made me a bit jittery. I mean, she is an almost qualified beauty therapist. What does she need to ask them? I thought. Then I heard hushed discussion playing out. Nothing I could make out, bar the odd words like 'dozy, stupid cow' and 'completely fucked'. Porsha came back in after and stood next to the bed.

'Right, Etta, babes. I ain't going to bullshit you, you're well in the shit,' Porsha informed me, covering me up from neck to toe with another towel.

'She's decent. Come in, girls,' called Porsha, sheepishly, as my eyes darted between her and Yana, Jenna and Carly.

'What are you all on about? Why am I in the shit? Is this a joke like when we told Nicky eyebrow dye lasted two years?' I asked, giggling.

'Umm, Etta, babes. No, this is not a wind-up. But don't panic. I'm gonna level with you, it's not coming off,' said Porsha while biting her lip.

'But you just said all the hair was off?' I reply, narrowing my eyes. At this point I have to say I wasn't that panicky, because I didn't fully understand the situation and was a bit tipsy.

'Yeah, I mean the wax, babes. I think it might be, well, it's definitely a bit well dodgy sort of thing.'

I ask what she means by a bit dodgy.

'Like I've yanked the strips and the hair has come off, but like all the wax didn't. And it's also sort of well stuck your, erm, you know, together. I think the problem is that I used some wax I picked up in a wholesaler's in Luton. I also think you have also had a bit of an allergic reaction. But at least the hair is off. That's something, hey!' Porsha replied. I could see Jenna mouthing, 'What now then?' at her.

'Sorry, what did you say? My what is stuck together?' I asked, processing the information. 'I don't get what you're saying.'

'Basically, mate, the dozy cow has used dodgy wax that has given you an allergic reaction, taken off some of your skin and also glued your fanny shut,' Jenna clarified.

Carly's eyes meet mine and she pulls an 'oh fucking hell face'.

'I think we need to try and get it off,' said Carly, stating the obvious.

I feel I should add that I was still pretty calm at this stage. All things considered. It was decided that Yana would ring Simon to pick her up and run her up Tesco before it shut. There she would grab supplies such as wax and hair remover, Sudocrem and lemon juice. I am not sure who thought of lemon juice, possibly Jenna as I vaguely remembered her telling us how it had helped her out of a jam after a tanning disaster.

I decline Porsha's suggestion of them all helping me lay 'fanny up' near the fire to avoid 'further setting'. But I accept the offer of another drink. But by the time Yana arrives back it would be a fair to say I am starting to feel a bit fucking panicky, to be honest with you.

I'm then cold waxed stripped, Veeted, and lemon bathed, but still covered in wax.

'I will ring Val! She's a nurse, she will know what to do!' Jenna declares after I made the huge mistake of shuffling off by myself into my bathroom with my make-up mirror to survey the damage. I now know the true meaning of the saying 'there are some things you cannot unsee'.

'Ring 111,' advises Val. 'You can't mess around where genitals are concerned.'

Jenna tells Porsha she needs to make the call, as she has 'seen it up close' and can 'explain the full'.

'Issue in full? I can explain the issue in full: my vagina looks like the inside of a butcher's bin! That's the issue in full!' I shout out, wondering if this is what an out-of-body experience feels like and downing another thimble of Ouzo.

Porsha dials 111. I'm not going to bullshit you, I was close to proper losing my shit by the time Porsha starts talking to Liz the call handler.

'Hiya, hun,' says Porsha without a care in the world. 'So the thing is my mate Etta has a bit of an issue with some wax. It's a bit sort of faulty and we need some information on how to sort of unstick her minge, oh, and also advice on what she can use to calm down the redness cos, as my mate said herself, it looks a bit like the inside of a butcher's bin at the minute, and she is due on a first date tonight with my mate's cousin and—'

Lizzie's non-fazed Geordie call handler cuts in. 'Oh dear. Okay. I need to ask your friend some initial questions, please,' says Lizzie. Yana takes the phone and puts it on speakerphone while I give her my name, address and date of birth.

'Right, I need to run through some questions. Are you bleeding?' asks Lizzie.

'Well a little because the wax has been taken the skin off in a small area—'

'Do you feel clammy to the touch?'

'Yes I am very clammy, because I am panicking.'

'Do you have any pains in your chest?'

'Now you come to mention it, yes, yes I have and I am also having heart palpitations which I am sure you'd agree is pretty fucking standard given my fucking labia is suck together and I mean proper fused. Oh god, I'm going to level with you, Lizzie. I need help. I am proper panicking.'

'Right, Miss Wilson, from your answers it is clear that you need an ambulance. Help will be with you soon.' My heart starts to beat even faster.

Jenna and Carly starts laughing. Like even more than us in the cafe with Yana. Ever the supportive friend and sister, I think, as Jenna announces that she is 'going to wet herself' whilst I try to protest with an adamant Lizzie.

'What, no! Honestly, Liz, I just need someone to tell me how to unstick my vagina. Just tell me how to get my labia apart!' I plead. Lizzie the call handler isn't having any of it.

'Sorry, but the computer has said you need urgent assistance and an ambulance has already been dispatched. Please have someone go downstairs and open a door, they will be with you soon.'

Oh Fucking Brilliant.

The paramedics who arrived wearing Santa hats were really good about it, although I don't think much of one of them saying they 'Couldn't wait to tell everyone about this one!' And the other laughing nearly as much as the pack of to borrow Maggie's well-loved phrase 'c u next Tuesdays' also known as my friends and sister had been throughout, only pausing while Yana announced: 'The paramedics for the poorly pussy has arrived!' when the room filled with the tell-tale blue flashing lights.

Thankfully, Aiden and Lennie also gave me a lotion that they kept handy for 'idiots that manage to superglue themselves together' which really did the job. It dissolved all the wax and some cooling gel, that Lennie said was usually used for severe burn victims, took away the redness and some of the inflammation.

'Now, don't worry, mate, I've texted Jas to let Richie know that you've got your period and so won't be up for any shaggin' later,' said Jenna.

'Why did you say that?' I moaned.

'Well I thought it was better than saying that your fanny currently resembles a punched lasagne. Lesser of two evils and all that, mate.' Fair point.

We couldn't get a taxi, so started making our way up the farm track as Carly made comments like, 'God, you're asking to be murdered you are, living somewhere like this, you mentalist!' My phone started to ring.

'Hello, darling, just a little reminder again about collecting the meat from the butcher's. Have you got it yet?' No? Right, well you need to get your skates on as they shut in forty-five minutes, darling.'

'Okay, I will go there now,' I reply. Fuck, I forgot all about promising to collect the turkey.

'Remember to ask for Zane, and tell him Pamela sent you. He gave me the best stuffing of my life last year, and so generous with the portions! Honestly, do you remember? So much meat! I've never been so full as in Christmas 2020.'

I promised that I was heading straight there now and would send Carly back with it after one quick drink.

But things didn't exactly go to plan.

CHAPTER 8

In hindsight, the last double Ouzo while I tried to get Lizzie, the NHS call handler, to cancel the paramedics was probably one too many.

Still, at least I made Yana and Carly laugh when I swung open the doors of Jones and Sons butcher's and declared I was: 'Here to collect my meat!' And then called at the top of my lungs, 'Zane? I have been told you must be my meat supplier. Zane, who gave my step-nan the best stuffing of her life, come hither!' Admittedly it sounded better in my head than the actual execution, because I started hiccupping and lost my balance when the floor starting moving, but Jenna said it got a lot of hearts on her Instagram Story.

I do feel I need to go on record now in case Pam is reading this and say I clearly also remember handing the bag of meat to Carly and saying, 'Now, Carly, this is an important bag of meat. You must return to our grandad's within the hour. Pamela needs Zane's meat.'

Carly later said she thought I was just 'fuckin' about'. But I wasn't, and she knew I wasn't.

So where were we? Right, we had unfused my labia, drunk nearly two litres of Ouzo and a bottle of cooking sherry I'd won at Chloe's school summer fayre between us and picked up Pam's important meat. We had headed over to The Axe and Compass, because Jase and Richie were in The Riverview, and I wanted to have one more drink 'for my nerves' and wanted Jenna to touch up my make-up. (Another fact I will add in here is that this was, in hindsight, another error. Jenna, although fantastic at make-up while sober/tipsy/fairly shitfaced, isn't really as good when really steaming drunk. She uses far too much lip liner and blusher. I have the (now untagged) Instagram photos to prove it.

So we're all having a little drink and Kylie Minogue's 'Santa, Baby' is playing. Before we know it, Jason and Richie have come looking for us because we have had quite a few more than just a few drinks. Then I notice that Porsha has gone, but Carly is still at the bar snogging a man in an Aston Villa shirt. I presume (if this is Pam reading) that she's already taken home the meat and came back out, to escape my mum and Nigel.

It's Christmas Eve, fair play, who can blame her.

Although I am a bit worried that Richie will prefer Carly to me when she bounds over and introduces herself because, well, as I've already told you, Cameron Diaz smile, very long limbs. A bit giraffe-like, really. But it's all worry over nothing as Richie barely looks up when Carly kisses him on the nose; I think she was aiming for the cheek though, quite possibly the lips. (Again, as I said, when you're imagining Carly think Sienna Miller but much sluttier.) It's a bit hazy from this point, but I do remember turning to Richie and saying, 'Do you like her more than me?' Oh god, I am such a knob. Richie, thank Christ, laughed, thinking I was actually joking.

'Nah, not really my thing.' So I then, having quite a considerable amount of Ouzo-based bravery behind me, leaned into him and asked, 'What is your thing then?' While chewing my hair. No, I have no idea either. But it must have looked sexy as he leaned into me and growled, 'You, you're my thing.'

We were still mid-passionate snog as Carly shouted right in my ear, 'Etta. Etta! Yana just asked me where did you put Pam's turkeys?'

'Where did I put them?' I shout back. 'What are you asking me where I put them for? *You* said you was taking the bag home!' I said accusingly to Carly.

'I did no such thing! You know Pam asked *you* to get the meat and not me. She *knows* I can't be trusted.' Carly and I then had a bit of a heated exchange of words where I called her 'useless and childish' and she told me to 'pipe down' and 'wind my neck in'.

Jenna came over to us then and asked what was wrong. When Richie explained the turkey had been misplaced, she helpfully laughed and said, 'You're both fuckin' screwed! Pam is going to lose her shit! She has been textin' me 'bout that turkey all month!' Yep, thanks, Jenna.

Jase then asked if we were sure we had lost it. 'Good point,' said Carly. 'Give me a bunk up then!' Carly said, already hitching herself up the bar.

'Erm excuse me! EXCUSE ME!' bellowed Carly, while making a megaphone shape with her hand over her mouth. 'Now, has anyone seen a bag of meat?'

Unsurprisingly, no one had. Still, it was an improvement on her last public speaking engagement when she managed to offend every guest who wasn't a blood or in-law relative of hers with one single question. (I'm also counting Nigel in this as had been deeply offended and I also don't count him as an in-law. He may claim not to recognise a marriage registered by the UK government or Church, but I personally refuse to recognise a marriage what is confirmed by a woman who declares 'you are man and wife you may imprint on each other's souls!' But that's a whole different story.)

Despite being really drunk, I was getting a bit panicky and asked Jenna if I should admit myself in hospital for PTSD after earlier 'events'.

'Pam might go easier on me if she thinks I am emotionally broken,' I said.

'This I doubt. The special bird was ordered in May,' Yana said. 'Pam told me at garden party. We decide to have another drink to decide what to do. Jase and Richie stand by the fruit machine with pints in their hands while we discuss.

'I could push you over and say we got mugged?' suggested Carly.

'Why don't I push you over and say you got mugged!' I replied at Carly, glaring at her. 'This is your fault! You have always been the same. Like when you borrowed my Fruit of the Loom jumper and left it at the school disco.'

'We were in primary school! Let it go!' Carly shouted back.

'God, you two could give aspirin a headache. Lucky for you I know what to do!' said Jenna, tapping her phone screen.

'Let's have one more drink here, then pop over to Tesco Express. I've Googled and it's open until nine. We can just buy some replacements. No problemo!' she told us smugly.

'Right, Jase, you and Richie look out for our taxi and us girls will run in, grab what we need, and meet you by the clock tower,' said Jenna confidently, after shit loads more than 'one more drink'.

When we got to Tesco express it was open, but not as well stocked as we had anticipated.

'Fuck,' I said, staring at the shelves like if I did something may magically appear. Jenna patted my arm.

'Leave this to me. No bother. It will be out the back, let's go and ask at the tills,' she said confidently.

The cashier was pulling down the shutters where the alcohol and cigarettes are stored when Carly stumbled forwards and held out her palm to Yana, Jenna and I.

'I'll handle this. Soooo, we need turkey, free-range if you have it, some meat suitable for the vegans, and a *really good* stuffing,' Carly announced to the twenty-something man behind the counter, who was twisting his lip piercing.

'There might be some pork chops left. I close in ten.' He said pointing in the vague direction of the fridge aisle.

It had started raining by the time we had paid and got into the taxi. Thank goodness Richie was there to help me up when the floor moved, twice in one night! What's with these floors? I do really wish I hadn't declared that I 'loved the feel of his beard against my cheek' and then tugged him down (Yes, by his beard) saying repeatedly, 'ummmm let me smell it!' Even Carly was doing the hand slicing neck gestures at me.

To be honest, at the time I was feeling pretty fucking good about our replacement dinner items, as we pulled up to Grandad and Pam's.

I know Carly was as well actually, as she kept getting the packet of Paxo out of the carrier bag and saying things like 'good buy that'. To no one in particular.

I think I fell asleep for a minute of two, and woke up with a startle thinking that I was either at Grandad's from the sudden blinding light, or that Pam had found out about the turkey and done me in in my sleep. Then I remembered we had our replacements. All would be fine.

'Bloody hell, wouldn't like the leckkie bill for this place!' the taxi driver said, reaching into his jean pocket to take a photo. Richie helped me and Carly inside while Jenna waved and gave us thumbs up from the window of the taxi.

Pam had stood with her mouth open, as Carly had held up her hand close to Pam's lips and made a 'sssshhh' noise.

'Pamela Wilson, *step this way*!' Carly said in a voice that reminded me of the man who used to call out contestants' names on the *Price is Right* game show.

Pam, to be fair to her, seemed amused by this and duly followed Carly and I into the kitchen. She didn't even moan when Carly threw the carrier bag onto the side and it landed in a plate of mince pies.

'Right, so a change of plan, Pam,' Carly said, looking to me for backup.

'Carly lost the meat, Pam,' I said sadly.

'We both lost it!' Carly cried. 'But we took responsibility and got replacements. Now, we couldn't get a turkey or even a chicken, but we did get these!' I said, pulling out a packet of Bernard Matthews Turkey Drummers.

'Delicious and cooks from frozen in 25–30 mins,' Carly added, grinning. 'And we even got these Cum-beer-land sausages,' Carly slurred, reading from the packet.

'With added herbs!' I add.

'For the vegans,' concluded Carly.

Pam is momentarily speechless.

'Oh very funny, you two!' chuckled Pam. But you can't fool me! It was me that opened the door when your lovely friend delivered my butcher's order, safe and sound, not that long ago actually,' said Pam, looking at her watch.

'What friend?' I asked

'You know, the one that had that little mishap with her work.'

'Porsha?' I said, confused.

'Yes, darling. She said she was going home for an early night. Looks like you two have had the same idea yourselves! No night with young man after all?' Pam asked, handing me a glass of Robinsons squash.

'No, it was too late,' I said, considering Porsha not only going home before me, but also bringing home my bags. I am out of control, I think, like proper out of control if I am out later than Porsha.

'Too late?' Pam scoffed 'It's half-past nine.' She titters. You only missed Chloe by an hour.

Told Carly I was going to get Grandad to drop me off at mine and pick Richie up on the way as we sat on the kitchen floor, waiting for the turkey drummers we had decided to cook.

'I'm not sure that's the best idea, Etta. I think you're a bit too pissed,' Carly said. I considered this for a moment, and then concluded that if Carly, the person that had just asked if I wanted to 'go for a swim' in Pam's koi carp pond while we waited for our food to cook, is telling me she thinks I am a bit too pissed, I most definitely am a bit too pissed.

Grandad and Pam went to bed then, to read their books, so Pam said we could lie on the sofas and relax as long as we promised to 'swap ends every hour, to avoid uneven wear'. A text from Richie arrived as we were watching *Gremlins*.

Had a good night, hope Pam liked her meat! (Laughing face) Can't wait to see you when we leave for Scotland. Happy Christmas, Etta. X

'First time he's put a kiss,' I told Carly.

'Must have been all that beard sniffing,' said Carly, chuckling. 'I can't believe you was tugging on his beard. You looked like a fuckin' bell-ringer.'

It wasn't the Christmas Eve I was expecting, but despite the lost-but-not-lost Christmas meat and the emergency services, it was the best one I've had in years.

CHAPTER 9

Christmas Day, St Ives, Cambridgeshire

There is something comforting and nostalgic about waking up in my childhood bedroom on Christmas morning, even as a hungover thirty-something adult. It's become a tradition. I usually have to work some of the festive period, and so we have fallen into a routine over the years, of Grandad picking me and Chloe up on Christmas Eve, Grandad carrying the Christmas sacks of full presents from under my tree into his boot.

It was a bit different this year, but Pam still greeted us with a chorus of 'Howard Blake' on the CD player, her in the reindeer apron she's had since the early 2000s. Wafts of still-warm sausage rolls escaping from the kitchen. My bedroom hasn't been decorated since 1993. The lava lamp next to the thirty-two-inch-wide screen brick of a television still blobs about and you can just about see the sun, moon and stars wallpaper beneath the sea of MN8 and Eternal posters.

I don't know why Pam hasn't redecorated my room ten times over by now; she certainly has in the rest of the house, including Carly's old bedroom which is now Chloe's bedroom. That room alone has been jungle-themed, princess and now My Little Pony. Chloe woke us all up with excited shrieks of 'He's been, he's been!' I had promised myself to treasure this Christmas, knowing that it could very likely be our last with Chloe being as Pam refers to as 'a believer'.

If it wasn't for the portable North Pole app (you must try it if you have children) and Grandad's very detailed fabrications of when he personally has spotted the North Pole on his telescope, she wouldn't have lasted this long. All of us adults have pledged not to open our presents until we get to Scotland, but we exchange stockings, apart from Carly, who's gone back to bed.

'Where's Mum and Nige?' I ask, suddenly realising we are two guests down.

'Coming Boxing Day now,' Grandad replied.

'Shame,' I said, smirking at Pam, who agreed it was, her face telling a different story.

I had decided not to worry about steps today and accepted Grandad's offer of a lift to work. Carers are like other health professionals. We need to work regardless. This year I got allocated a Christmas Day shift of 3pm until 11pm, which I didn't mind. We left early enough to be able to pop into my landlord Tom's with a plate of dinner. Tom always declines my offer of joining us each year, but gladly accepts the still-hot plate of turkey and all the trimmings, I call in with.

I have a bit of flashback on the way round, to yesterday evening as the plate heat surges into my thighs. I am so thankful Porsha has had some kind of personality transplant and went home early, dropping the turkey in to Pam on the way. Not sure Tom would have enjoyed a Paxo ball and single turkey drummer as much as the piled luxury feast I have for him.

We've gotten into a routine over the years: Tom collects Alice, my Ragdoll cat, who he adores nearly as much as she does him, on Christmas Eve, and looks after her until Boxing Day evening when I return home to the cottage. He seemed chuffed when I asked if there was a possibility of him also looking after her while we went on our trip to Scotland.

Nicky was taking off her coat as I walked into the staff room.

'Happy Christmas, Nic!' I said. As soon as Nicky turned around, I could tell she wasn't her usual upbeat self.

'Merry Christmas, have you had a good day? Did Chloe like her new skates?' she replied through a strained smile.

'She did, yes. I've had a lovely day. What about you?' I ask, but before Nicky can answer Porsha, Jenna and Val bustle in draped in tinsel.

'And I said to him, Jase, mate, I don't care. You have a pair of arms, two working hands; you can wrap your own sodding family's presents! I bought it for ya. I ain't wrapping it as well! Alright, you two? Merry Christmas!' Jenna giggles, draping her leather jacket over the back of a chair. We all exchange chitchat on how our days have been. Val has had an awkward lunch with her, Adonis and her son. 'I'm glad to have had to come to work to be honest with you all. You could cut the tension with a knife. It seems having a father who marries the man he'd been cheating on his mother with for years is fine, but his mum finding happiness with an old friend isn't,' Val tells us, shaking his head.

'I know that feeling,' mutters Nicky, flicking on the staff kettle, picking up a tea towel and vigorously drying mugs from the draining board. Val asks Nicky how her day had been.

'Well, not great to tell the truth. I feel a bit in the way. And my son won't come round while they are there, he says,' Nicky said as she scoops a heaped spoon of coffee into each of the four mugs.

'How can you be in the way in your own bloody house, mate?' Jenna asked while passing a carton of long-life milk.

'Well, it's like I am not there. I don't know, probably me being silly, maybe it's just because I am so out of practice of sharing my home with anyone else.'

'Was your dinner nice at least?' I ask, gently blowing on my piping-hot drink.

'I haven't had it yet,' Nicky said sheepishly.

'Me either, babes, I was so hungover I couldn't face it. Had no headache pills either, so I've been struggling all day. Did you remember to bring some paracetamol, Jen, babes?' Porsha asks.

'Oh, by the way, thank you for dropping my bag of meat off, lifesaver,' I say to Porsha. Porsha tells me it's the least she could do after the situation.

'You went home early, how are you hungover?' Yana asks, narrowing her eyes at Jenna, pulling out the six plus Calpol box from her bag and handing two to Porsha. 'Only thing I had, mate,' Jenna said apologetically.

'I went home and got on the Malibu with my mum. Thanks, babes,' Porsha said, accepting the box. 'Do you want some if you're feeling ropey, Nic?' offered Porsha, lifting the bottle out of the red box.

'No, no, I'm not ill, thank you. It's nothing like that. Dot… Matt's mum doesn't like to eat her Christmas dinner until four, that's all.'

'So let me get this straight. You've not had a Christmas meal?' Val asked, narrowing her eyes at the rest of us.

"That you paid for!' chimes in Jenna in sheer outrage. 'Nah. No, gone too far now, mate!'

Val starts furiously shaking her head and asks, 'Are you telling us that you haven't had the meal that have planned and paid for because the guests in YOUR house wanted to eat an hour after you started work?' Nic nods her head, biting her lip.

'They're taking the fucking piss, mate!' fumes Jenna

'What did Matt say? In fact, what did you say? Why did not you say, "Well actually that's tough tits because I am working all day from three so I will be having my lunch when I want it and if you don't want it, don't fuckin eat it!' Jenna rants, not unkindly.

'Oh well. You know how I am. And Matt just said his mum has always eaten Christmas dinner at four and that she would save some to eat when I got back.'

'That's good of her. So you will be warming up leftovers at eleven o'clock tonight?' I ask.

'Least they'll be going home tomorrow, mate. You live and you learn. Don't invite them again,' says Porsha, while Jenna is firing off a text, which receives a reply a few seconds later.

'Fuck em, mate. Mum's dishing you a plate now for Jase to shoot round with. We had shitloads and it will still be hot cos Nana borrowed some silver buffet hot plates for the leftovers. You can make some gravy in the kitchen. We still have ten minutes till shift anyway.'

Nicky says there is no need, but thanks Jenna and admits that she is 'rather peckish' after only having had beans on toast 'early this morning' and her not having time to have lunch; she'd been too busy peeling the vegetables for her guests' dinner.

'Can one of you lot help me with this lid before we start, please? It's stuck,' said Porsha, holding out the medicine bottle.

I take the bottle and giggle. 'It's not stuck, it's a child lock,' I tell her, pushing down the lid and twisting it open.

'Ain't technology clever! It must have thought I was under sixteen, that's why I couldn't open it! I keep telling you to have some Botox, don't I, Etta babes.'

I consider bringing Porsha up to speed, but then a smirking Jenna caught my eye; she scrunched her nose and shook her head in a 'don't even bother' gesture.

'Sometimes, Etta, ignorance really is bliss,' said Val, glancing over at Nicky who was now in the small wall office mirror wrapping green tinsel around her head like a halo. 'Until it isn't,' I say.

Val nods and sucks in her lip.

'Fucking Matt. I knew he was a wrongun,' raged Jenna under her breath in a low voice as we left our handover. Which she did, but then we all had concerns. The problem is we can all have the concerns and opinions in the world, but as Val pointed out, it is Nicky's life and we can only say so much.

Least Nic enjoyed the rest of her day. We all did, in fact. Jenna played 'resident DJ', blasting out Christmas songs from her phone and portable speaker for the livelier residents who, as Jenna said, 'wanted to paaarrttaaayyy!'

Porsha based herself in the crafts room, spending time chatting to some of her book club members who really seem to be enjoying living vivaciously through her. Every time I passed the doors I heard things like 'Well I never!' And 'And what is The Tinder? Can I get it on my smart television?'

For residents that wanted a quieter day we took snacks and drinks to their rooms, after the medication rounds, and Nicky popped in to everyone for a 'cheery chat'. While Val, always the best with tears, held a 'remembering circle' for those struggling or missing loved ones and wished to share stories and memories of happier times.

Bit depressing to be honest with you, as lovely as it is for residents to have the chance to share their stories, but as Porsha pointed out, Val is in such high spirits probably due to 'All the shaggin' with her Greek god.' It would take a lot to affect her morale. And all the residents seem to perk up once they've stopped crying, some even joining us for games in the dining room.

As the evening drew in, a game of charades is organised by Reg.

Reg always looks forwards to Christmas. Correction: Reg always looks forward to his Christmas whisky, that his son-in-law drops in to him every Christmas morning, together with a bulging hamper of goodies.

From his animated performance as he takes his turn, I suspect Reg has made a good dent in the bottle already. By the time he has wriggled about on the floor for a few minutes, shaking his head frantically, when come guesses of *Celebs on Ice* and *The Bill* from Joannie, who, it seems, hasn't quite grasped the one word and film part of the game.

Reg then, after pulling himself up off of the floor again, starts to do a weird motion with his arms above his head, he then holds his leg and lets out a soundless scream.

'Fuck, is he havin' an attack?' Porsha asks me with genuine concern. I reassure her he is fine.

None of us have got the first clue, despite the five minutes of solid miming Reg has put in. It appears Reg had given up as he got up and walked off, disappearing down the hall with a tut and dismissive wave of his hand.

Margaret is just deciding if her book is four words or five, when Reg bounds back through the door, a bottle of Heinz tomato ketchup, that he keeps in his room for pie and chip Tuesday, tucked under his arm.

Reg takes to the floor again, snaking about and rolling around in no particular fashion. For a second I am worried that Porsha is right and he is having a fit of some kind. I'm just considering asking him if he is alright when Reg heaves himself onto his arthritic knees and crawls over to his chess partner, Fred.

'Roll up ya trouser leg, Fred, ole boy!' Reg instructs. As soon as his friend follows his instructions, Reg leans down towards Fred's leg, squirts ketchup all over it, and then pretends to sink his teeth into his shin.

'I know, I know!' shouts Joanie. 'I've seen it on Sky at my daughter's! *The Walking Dead*!'

'Do keep up, Joanie,' said Margaret, her voice as patronising as ever. 'One word film! He is clearly eating a person and therefore the answer is Hannibal,' she says smugly. Bloody good guess that.

'I was going to say *Holby City*,' said Olive. 'Wasn't that an excellent series? Do you all know that it was not a real hospital, nor real doctors?'

'You lot are fucking useless! I've been swimming round this floor, getting covered in digestive crumbs and pine needles for the last ten minutes! *And* I've just taken a chunk out of my mate's leg! *And* used at least a quid's worth of ketchup as props! It's bloody *Jaws*, you pack of fools! Jaws! I was being a fucking shark!'

A chorus of 'Language!'; 'oh was that what that was'; and the odd: 'Oh, yes!' Is still in full flow when Reg turns to Porsha and me and says, 'No wonder I drink!'

CHAPTER 10

Boxing Day, St Ives, Cambridgeshire

On Boxing Day, I got back to Grandad and Pam's just after one, and was in my cuddly new onesie that Pam had given me in my 'Stocking', which was the size of a bin bag.

Had a really chilled afternoon scoffing turkey sandwiches and watching *Elf* with Chloe. Pam, who had been up and dressed by quarter to five, had offered me a lift to work, calling in to withdraw cash. When I asked her what she needed three hundred pounds in twenty-pound notes for, thinking maybe Grandad had really stepped up the binman bribery, she told me she planned to send Carly off to the Boxing Day sales to buy some new clothes 'that have sleeves.' For our trip to Scotland.

Carly returned laden with bags, just after three in the afternoon, but judging by the various Hawaiian Tropic tanning oils and various skimpy bikinis that Carly had flaunted about in whilst Pam sat pursed lipped, shaking her head, she hadn't done as Pam had instructed and thought 'would I wear this in the North Pole?' Even once before heading to the checkout.

I can't say I was that surprised that Carly then, after getting an IOU from Grandad, had booked a flight somewhere hot and off she went to Luton airport via a lift, also from Grandad. Gillian called round just as Chloe gone to bed and I had settled down with a selection box (don't panic, I'm not off the wagon; I only had a *Freddo*!). They completely took over the dining room for 'last checks', as they kept referring to their manic list-ticking. When my grandad returned, he asked Pam if her and Gillian *really* needed to go through all of the suitcases, boxes and bags again.

'To fail to prepare is to prepare to fail,' Pam had replied smugly. Nearly said that that wasn't always true. That I prepared my room, even buying a new shaggy rug (the name it came with, by the way, not one I'd given it) although I could see the irony and my plan ended in me drunk on a sofa eating processed turkey with my sister.

Pam asked me if I had watched the YouTube video on how to splint a leg and make a stretcher out of plaited leaves yet. I started gaffing then, and said a bit smugly, 'I think you're forgetting, we have an ex-SBS soldier at our disposal. You know Richie, my boyfriend?'

'Darling, I know it's exciting to have a real-life boyfriend, especially one that can climb up ladders and change lightbulbs, but as Gilly pointed out last week, what if he falls to his death and leaves us all in the lurch, stranded and fractured? No, darling, we need to all take responsibility and learn basic survival skills. I am gathering also then you have also yet to make fire? From the flint I gave you on Wednesday? Really, Henrietta, you need to get with the programme, darling, doesn't she, Gilly?'

'You do. I have watched enough *Monarch of the Glen* to know that The Highlands can be a beautiful but cruel mistress,' said Gilly, giving me a look full of judgment.

I promised to pack a warmer coat and asked Jenna to bring me one of her Zippos.

'There's no place for facetiousness in the Scottish wilderness. At least watch an episode of Bear Grylls, darling,' Pam said in a strained voice.

I rang Richie to relay the conversation to him, so we could have a giggle about it, but he didn't laugh. He just went quiet, then said, 'To be honest, Etta, they're right, it's one thing being in a cosy cottage with the heating on, the cupboards stocked and the fire roaring, but it's another if you venture out. It is a wilderness out there, especially this time of the year. If you don't have supplies and the right kit, you could find yourself in a world of shit.' I wanted Richie to know that I was taking it seriously, so told him that I had packed some heavy-duty wellies wear when I walk the corgis and that I had also borrowed some earmuffs and very fluffy faux mink Russian-style hat from Yana. He belly-laughed for a really long time, then wheezed, 'I've heard it all now! You'll be telling me that you've downloaded a compass on ya phone next! You do make me laugh. Can't wait to see ya in the morning though. I've had no one smelling my beard for days now.' As we said our goodbyes I heard him chuff the word 'earmuffs' and start chuckling again to himself as he ended the call. Have just deleted the where am I? compass app. Although it seemed perfectly reliable to me.

How many lists do you think someone who is in co-charge of arranging a five-day trip for sixteen people to the Scottish Highlands needs? Well, I can't tell you the answer to that exactly, but I can tell you how many lists Pam has made, who is in co-charge. Forty-three. That's right, four three: 43!

Some examples at random for you:

1. Suitcase Pamela pack list.
2. Suitcase Edward (my grandad).
3. Etta suitcase (as I am incapable of packing own suitcase at the age of thirty).
4. Chloe's suitcase (see above).
5. Dogs wheelie and coats (corgis do not travel light).
6. Cleaning list for house before leave.
7. Neighbour response emergency numbers (Pam, despite living in street where a crisp packet being dropped is considered a major event, the residents all go on 'high alert' when one of them spend more than five hours away from their house).
8. List of numbers for coach hire, owner of rented lodge, AA breakdown (despite us not travelling by car, and Pam also having the number programmed in hers, mine and her co-organiser Gillian's mobile phones).
9. Check status of Ocado shop that is due to arrive between 6–7am, together with a checklist of essential listed items not available and send my grandad to collect those from Sainsburys.
10. Ask Etta if she needs any family planning support in her bedroom and provide if needed. Oh god, no.
11. Possible songs to set the mood on executive coach.
12. Possible songs for luxury lodge.
13. Possible breakfast, lunch and dinner topics for a well-rounded and non-offensive chats. (Check if

we can mention views on dolphin friendly tuna in front of Hilary and Nigel.)
14. Food items for executive coach.
15. Beverage items for executive coach.
16. Clean-up and sick-prevention items for executive coach to be placed near Maggie and her mother. (Gillian's handwriting.)
17. Seating plan suggestions for executive coach.
18. Words not to be used around little ears whilst in executive coach and luxury lodge.
19. Vegan-friendly items for the vegans.
20. Activities suitable for all the guests (even the vegans): horse-riding, whisky-tasting (age limits apply), walking, pub and watching squirrels (red and endangered).
21. Activities possibly suitable for all (even the vegans.) Fly-fishing? Is this vegan-friendly if we throw them back in?
22. Bedroom allocation list.
23. Must-dos before leaving house: defrost freezer, bleach wheelie bins, triple-check timer on lights, turn blinds to semi-closed upstairs, full closed downstairs, place phone chargers, spare phone chargers, first-aid kit, defibrillator and epi pen in safe place in executive coach.
24. Local hospitals and ensure everyone knows the emergency number is 999 in case of any confusion. (This should also be laminated and handed to guests upon entry to lodge.)
25. Hosts to perform a count of guests at breakfast and bedtime in case we lose some of them in the Highlands or pub.

26. Remember to re-charge walkie-talkies and always carry them on person.

Can't be arsed to write anymore. You get the picture.

11p.m. The same evening, St Ives, Cambridgeshire

Mum and Nigel arrived four hours later than scheduled. Well, three days if you count the fact they were originally due on Christmas Eve.

Commer, Nigel's VW camper van, which although isn't old enough to be put into vintage category, is without doubt enough of a wreck to be well and slotted into the shit heap on wheels one alerted us to its arrival, squealing and crunching as Nigel reversed it next to the family Picasso.

Grandad and Pam had both rushed out in their matching his and hers dressing gowns to greet them. I reluctantly followed behind and hovered at the doorstep.

'We thought you'd got lost! We'd given up and gone to bed!' chortles Pam in her jokey 'I am joking, but also not joking' voice.

'Yeah, man, we had to stop on the M11 to send some healing across the plains to my friend's run over cat. He wasn't ready to go, was he, sweetheart.'

Mum doesn't say anything.

'An old soul who hadn't finished his tasks. Still, he passed peacefully once we arranged his next vessel, didn't he, sweetheart?' I push out my bottom lip and shrug at my grandad. Standard.

My grandad looks away and I let out a little laugh which I try to disguise with a yawn.

'I didn't know you could talk to the animals!' said Pam. I think she's probably taking the piss. 'Perhaps you could have a chat with Charles and Diana and let me know when puppies are on the cards!' she says, turning to head back inside.

'I spoke to both of them at length already, last time we was down. They have said some things…' said Nige. Pausing to add drama. God, no one's voice has made me want to punch them in the face as much as his does. Ever so fucking cocky. No one likes a self-important weirdo, do they?

'What kind of things?' Pam asks, stopping dead and not quite hiding her defensive tone. She sounds like a mother at the door of a pre-school when the teacher asks 'for a quick word'.

'Oh I couldn't say, man, it wouldn't be fair to my clients,' Nigel said, sliding open Commers' side door and climbing inside.

'Clients? They're dogs! I am their owner. Surely I have a right to know?' Pam countered, even more put out.

'They actually mentioned that. You have to accept you are part of the problem, Pam. You don't own them. None of us own anyone, or anything, only our own souls. It's about social acceptance and ownership, man.' Someone get this knob a straitjacket.

'They are Kennel Club registered and in my name,' Pam replies, the frosty look in her eyes enough to have Grandad scrambling to change the subject.

'Well, it's nice to have you both joining us for this little holiday anyway,' said Grandad diplomatically while giving me the 'I know and agree but leave it' face when I say, 'what a load of bollocks' to Pam quietly, but loud enough for Nigel to pop his head out the side of his shit heap and say, 'Sorry, I didn't hear what you said?'

Oh, I think you did.

Nigel wastes no time in wafting a smoking sage stick around the front garden and waving his hands about to set up a 'protective web of light'.

'Are you sure you don't want us to get the blow-up bed out of the garage, your dad could set it up in lounge?' Pam offers my mum. 'It's supposed to hit minus one tonight.'

'No thanks, we will fire up Jenny the genie,' Nigel replies before my mum can open her mouth as he lugs a very rusty mental generator out of the camper van.

Fast forward ten minutes and it sounds like a funfair or children's bouncy castle birthday party. What makes it worse is that the road is deathly quiet, so it is echoing. Pam is beside herself because a few houses' lights have gone on. Her main concern being that she will removed from the Willow Road residents Facebook chat group and then 'spoken about'.

'It happened to Suzie in the bungalow. They don't muck about and once you're out, that's it. There's no getting back in. Suzie's name was mud over those hanging baskets. I mean, she did bring it on herself, because she knew the colour scheme was not a guide, and she also knew how those pansies would go down; but even so, the names they called her. Gosh, no. I can't stand by and let *them* ruin my reputation. Something must be done!'

Pam instructs my Grandad to demand the generator is disconnected. My grandad points out that it is 'quite nippy out', but Pam couldn't care less. This is her access to the Willow Road private Facebook group on the line here!

'*They* can either come inside like normal human beings or *they* can unplug the Mary and Joseph Nativity scene from the outside electrical socket and borrow the plug-in blow heaters,' replied Pamela with a determined 'this is not a discussion' expression.

'Those heaters have been in the garage since 2001, when the boiler packed up.' Grandad pointed out. 'I'm just not sure they would be safe, Pamela, they could set the van on fire.' Pam rolled her eyes dismissively.

'You'll have to give them the fire extinguisher out of the kitchen then. Oh hell! Number 13 is looking out of their window. Hurry up, Edward! And you can also remind them they are not to use our compost heap as a toilet like they did last time!'

CHAPTER 11

Monday 27th December, St Ives, Cambridgeshire

Gillian and Barnaby arrived at five am on the dot. Pam, who had been up since four, bathing the corgis, tonging her hair and then pacing from room to room with her clipboard, her tartan Radley bumbag swishing relentlessly against her navy Barbour wax jacket, announced their arrival and darted out to great them.

'*Oh yes*!' said Pam, sounding like the woman on the dodgy hair advert a few years back. 'Oh, you two look adorable, Gilly, darling. Very Her Royal Highness Queen Elizabeth and Prince Philip Duke of Edinburgh, Balmoral 1986,' Pam gushed as she ushered them into the gleaming kitchen, the smell of Illy coffee merging into the Zoflora that had been used to scrub, wipe and mop every surface, as Pam plunged down the silver-plated cafetière; Harrods and therefore reserved for the most prestigious of guests/bad news and so forth.

'Thank you, Pammy. As do you both. See, Barnaby, Pammy is also wearing a silk headscarf! And I cannot hear Edward whining about wearing a very exclusive Troy London field gilet in brown tweed and the same Dubarry Galway boots as the Duchess of Cambridge practically lives in! I *told* you that's what *they* all wear in the Scottish Highlands!' said Gillian, opening a Coffee Mate carton and tipping it into her bone china cup.

'We reside in Cambridgeshire, Gillian! We're going on a short break. I don't see the need for all this extravagance! I had a perfectly good pair of Dunlop Wellingtons and three Regatta fleeces in the wardrobe. They would have done the same job for seven hundred pounds less!'

Pamela gives Gillian a 'he knows not what he says' look.

'And, for the record, none of us look like royals, but we do all look like berks,' adds Barnaby, gulping down his scolding hot coffee and huffing loudly.

My grandad mutters something about 'not being worth the upset' and suggests Barnaby give him a hand to load the car. It had been decided that Gillian and Barnaby would follow in 'the landie'. When I asked why, Pam had said it was so we had a 'set of safe wheels' when we got to Scotland. Which sounded feasible enough. Although I personally think it was the bus journey on Jenna's hen-do that put Gillian off. All the drinking and the dancing. But Chloe and Jenna and Jason's boys are coming on this trip, and so there won't be any of that. Well maybe from Jenna's nana. But then, as she said herself, 'I'm in my seventies, if I want to wear the same dress as Molly Mae from *Love Island*, have a few drinks and dance on the tables, I will do and anyone that don't like it needn't look.'

When I pop back downstairs to find my ringing phone, I hear Gillian and Barnaby in the hallway. Gillian is asking him in a low, strained voice to 'remember his promises' and reminding him he is in no place to 'have an opinion' given the 'recent events and revelations'.

Must ask Jenna about that! Whatever all that is about, it was enough to prompt Barnaby to backtrack and apologise for his 'uncalled for grumbles'.

When I check whose call I had missed, I see it's my mum's number so I call her back, despite her only being on the driveway.

'Etta. Can you tell your grandfather that him and his friend have woken me up with their sodding chatter chatter chatter and his wife's fucking strobe light strapped on her forehead! What on earth is going on? Poor Nige thought he had passed over in his slumber.' I can't help but titter at this. 'Oh I am glad it amuses you, Henrietta! I am a spiritual healer. None of you know the energy that is drained from me daily. Just no idea at all, have you? The living, the dead – you all want a piece! I don't stand a chance without my rest. I need my eight hours! So tell them to shut the fuck up!' she barks, hanging up. Very namaste.

Before I went out to pass on my mum's message, I make Chloe, who's now awake and downstairs, some toast. With Chloe settled in front of Nickelodeon, I head outside, like the good messenger girl I am. I can't help but stop dead, my brow furrowing at the sight that greets me, laughter escaping from deep in my chest. Pam and Gillian are standing side by side, in matching jackets, bumbags and headscarves, looking like two coal miners sponsored by Barbour.

'Oh, Gilly, darling, these head torches were an excellent buy! They've earned their money already!' said Pam, supervising my grandad and Barnaby lug half of Outdoors Adventures megastore from the house 'Careful of the wallpaper!' Then, staggering the five paces down the driveway, 'Do be careful of the paintwork!' (Pam)

'Being paid for in full, doesn't make it scratch and dent proof!' (Gillian) and into the car boot.

'Oh, I nearly forgot to tell you, Gilly,' said Pam, leaning down to pick up a takeaway flyer that has blown into the hedge at the side of the house. 'I logged onto the Gmail app this morning, and Veronica, the lodge owner, had replied! She said that, yes, the kitchen does have high-quality tea towels, but I've packed eight of mine, just to be on the safe side. Veronica also said that she hasn't been able to find us a pack of gun dogs to rent, but she will lend us her father-in-law's dogs. Two springer spaniels, a labrador, and a cocker-poo; it's a cross breed, but we can put him at the back.' Gillian breaks into a broad grin.

'Oh excellent, Pammy, that is good news. And good thinking on the tea towel front. Can't be too careful.'

I am just about to relay my Mum's message, and ask why they're renting dogs when we are taking (for our sins) Pam's corgis, Charles and Diana, along with Gillian's frisky Pomeranian, Captain or Captain James when he's being scolded by Gillian for 'being naughty' or 'doing naughties' to cushions, Diana's favourite squeaky pig, Pamela's new white fluffy slippers (which very unfortunately had an open toe) and, well, anything else that happens to give poor Captain James the horn. But then the coach pulled up, air brakes letting off a huge oosshhhhhh noise as the doors open and everyone clambers on, and excited chaos descends.

Jenna, who's still in her flannel pjs, the candy-pink baggy bottoms tucked inside her beige Ugg boots, pulls me in for a hug.

'I ain't even had a fag yet. I can't cope with being up this early and the kids before a fag,' says Jenna. 'Do us a favour, Gill, mate. Watch the kids for five minutes for me.' Gillian tuts, but duly heads over to her grandkids, who are standing at the end of the garden in puffa jackets and wellies, their heads buried in matching Nintendo switches.

Richie appeared and kissed me on the cheek.

'You look gorgeous. Although I was hoping to see your earmuffs!' He chuckled as I smiled and rolled my eyes. 'Just going to give everyone a hand with the kit,' said Richie, gesturing to Barnaby struggling with a stack of cardboard boxes marked as 'electric blankets'.

I stood with Jenna as she took long, thoughtful drags on the cigarette smouldering between her fingers.

'Where's your mum, then?' she asked as she took in the scene.

'Can you see the weed-covered *Ghostbuster*-type van?'

Jenna nods.

'Well that's where my mum and Nige, aka Kim Russo and John Bishop, are re-charging their auras as we speak.'

Jenna turns her head sideways to read the text.

'Fuckin' hell!' Jenna says, taking the words out of my mouth as it suddenly clicks, and I realise that the painted mural of a man in a white robe, lanky brown hair down to his shoulders, his arms raised and palms up either side of his face, who I thought last night was Jesus, is actually supposed to be Nigel.

'Look, Jen! It says medium and crystal healing on side. Can they, like, see dead people, then?' asked

Maggie, me joining in the conversation after she had come over to 'borrow a fag' from Jenna.

'So they say, but I very much doubt it,' I replied.

'Etta's worried about spending time with her mum and her new husband. Well, sort of husband. Remember I told you about the wedding they had in Cornwall?' asked Jenna, stubbing out what was left of her fag, and placing the dog end in the green bin.

'I do remember, yeah, and Jen did tell me all about your mum. So, Etta,' Maggie says, giving me a pointed look. 'If she gives you any shit, just say the word and I'll have her for you.' Thanked Maggie for her offer of physical violence against my mother.

'Oh is your sister here? Me and her got on like a house on fire, right top bird she is.' Asked Maggie.

'No, Carly fucked off on Boxing Day to Cape Verde. Judging by her Instagram posts, she's currently getting fucked via an honesty bar on the beach and a twenty-eight-year-old mature engineering student, who recently changed his name from Tom to Thunder via deed poll.

'Fair play,' said Maggie, nodding in approval. Cracking place, Cape Verde. Got off my tits a few times there myself as it goes.'

It hadn't taken long to get the coach loaded up. Not the way Richie had been effortlessly lifting armfuls of bulging suitcases. The second time Richie had passed me on the driveway, I was pretending to listen to Nigel, who had finally fell out of the back of the camper van and was droning on about how we would all die without funghi. Not the most absorbing of topics, so I'm sure I can be forgiven for allowing my mind and eyes to wander to

Richie as Nigel preached on about how 'funghi is the earth's miracle worker'.

In reflection I possibly was gawping a bit too adoringly in Richie's direction. But he was wearing grey tracksuit bottoms. If you know, then you know.

'Alright?' Richie said, giving me an amused grin as he strode towards me. Before I could answer, guess what he did? He lifted me up with one arm and with one swoop, he had pulled into him and planted a kiss on my cheek! I felt like Tarzan and Jane. For once me being Jane and not Tarzan.

It was a bit embarrassing, because everyone turned around to look, thanks to Jason shouting, 'Oi, oi, get a room!' At the top of his lungs. Embarrassing, but also brilliant. Then I noticed Chloe, who had come outside to play with Jenna's boys, eyeing Richie and me up. Felt a bit worried and anxious then as well, because although she knows Richie from FaceTime, she hadn't seen him *with* me and because it has always just been her and me.

I did have a chat with her a few days ago, and she'd said she didn't mind 'Mummy having a friend that's a boy'. But what you think you will feel about a situation, compared with how you actually do feel when you're in a situation, can be a lot different, can't it?

I have been fretting about it a lot, actually. But so far, so good. Richie must have also noticed Chloe staring at us, and guess what he did? He put me back down and strode over to Chloe and gestured for her to high-five him, which she did with a wide smile. Then Richie asked her what she got for Christmas.

'Oh wow, what colour is your new bike, then? Could I have a quick spin on it before we set off?' he asked a now-giggling Chloe.

'Big kid himself, that one,' Jenna's nana said, nodding towards Richie, as she dashed off to 'spend a penny' before we set off.

'I thought there were toilets on the coach,' I asked Jenna and Maggie as they stood next to the coach, having 'just one more quick puff'.

'There are, Etta, mate, yeah,' said Maggie, lowering her voice. 'But Mum don't trust them, not after that misunderstanding with the loo on the Gatwick Express. Blue hands and face she had for most of Magaluf. Looked like bloody David Dickinson and a Smurf had a love child, she did. Jenna, didn't your nana look like a Smurf love child when she got confused with the buttons on the train?' Jenna pushes her lips out and nods.

'The miserable sods wouldn't even wouldn't let her into the English breakfast cafe in case she was radioactive. You know, health and safety and all that shit. Poor cow was mortified, sitting on that wall outside waiting for us, weren't she, Jen? What was the song those kids were taunting her with? The one that goes Da-ba-dee-da-ba- di?'

'Eiffel 65, "I'm Blue",' said Jenna. Maggie shook her head as we burst into machine gun laughter.

'Don't let your nana hear you making jokes about it, madam. And you wouldn't been laughing if it had been you in Wilkos the other month. Did Jen tell you about that, Etta, mate?'

I shook my head. 'No, what happened?' I asked

'My nana had a panic attack after she picked up Duck toilet gel aqua instead of pine. 'Had to sit with her head between her knees in the aisle breathing into a pick n mix bag,' Jenna told me as she shook, as loud hoots escape her again.

'So traumatic it was,' said Maggie, shaking her head at the memory.

'Do be careful of the 22 plate Range Rover Discovery, boys! It may be top of the range with heated seats, television, privacy glass and satellite navigation system, but that doesn't mean it is immune from damage! It's no good, Pammy, either the life raft or the spare box of flares will have to stay here. Decisions need to be made, darling.'

'God, I almost forgot how fucking annoying she is!' Jenna was pulling a face and mimicking Gillian squawking at my grandad and Barnaby.

Maggie, who had just accepted a bacon sandwich from the tray Pamela had pranced past with, chimed in with a mouthful of food and brown sauce on her chin. 'That c u next Tuesday needs to learn some f'ing basic manners. Bloody bossing us all about. She told me I must try and watch my language when I was in the kitchen before, she wants to worry about herself.' Maggie said, expect she didn't say see you next Tuesday. Well she did, just not in those words, precisely. A short while after, dogs had been crated and very last wees had been tried for, Nigel had presented the coach driver with a protection bracelet, while my mum had tried to flog Bach Flower remedy to Jenna's nana, who was initially enthusiastic, then lost interest fast when Mum had confirmed that there wasn't any alcohol content in them, and couldn't also be 'downed like a shot'. And we were instructed by Gillian to line up to be head-counted, once by herself and then double-checked by Pamela. 'Lessons learned from *Home Alone*,' Richie had murmured into my ear, the beginnings of a wry grin appearing from under his beard.

The coach was certainly executive. Spacious with leather seats and futuristic lights, the blacked-out windows were framed with emerald-green curtains. There was even a little toilet at the back.

The kids, having had an early start and a good dose of early morning air, had cosied down with blankets to watch their Kindle Fires. They looked like mini pilots with their brightly coloured cordless headphones flashing in unison. There was a bit of a delay once we had all boarded. We all sat looking at each other as Pam stood at the front of the coach, holding her walkie-talkie in her hand, waiting for the 'all-clear' from Gillian.

'Come in, Camilla, Rightful Queen, this is Mrs Mountbatten? Do you receive me over?'

'I do, Mrs Mountbatten!' Pam shouts back into the walkie-talkie.

'I can confirm we are at the Co-op. Roads are clear. We now await Camilla Rightful Queen to pass. Do you receive over? No, no! Captain Naughty! Stop doing naughties with your new shawl!'

'I received you, Mrs Mountbatten, stand by,' said Pamela into the walkie-talkie.

Richie and I swap amused looks as Pam clips the handset back onto her waistband. 'Driver, you may begin our voyage to the Scottish Highlands. Please press play on playlist three, titled journey hours one to four, hashtag hopeful and excited!' said Pam, turning on her heels and striding towards her seat while giving us all a thumbs up gesture.

'Do that again, Pamela! Let's get a snap!' Jenna calls to Pam, who was only too happy to oblige.

CHAPTER 12

En Route to the Scottish Highlands

By the time we had joined the motorway towards Peterborough, Jenna's post of Pam in her Teresa May thumps up stance with the hashtag PamforPm has over two hundred hearts on Instagram.

'How do you know so many people?' Pamela asks Jenna, her eyes lighting up as Jenna scrolls slowly though the comments.

'They think I'm brilliant!' Pam calls over to Grandad, while holding up her phone. 'Wait until I show Gilly!'

It was just after Doncaster, when Nigel made his way, barefoot, up the aisle.

'Pamela, man, could I, like, change the tunes?' he slurred, like the words were just a bit too much effort for him. Grandad asked Nigel what he had in mind.

'I have some windpipe chill out, which may like totally clear the energy and we could all do some like group meditative soul-searching?' Nigel continues. Pam says nothing, but swings out her legs to form a protective barrier between Nigel and the music dock.

'Thank you, but I'm going to say no at the moment, and I'll tell you why. Wham and Shakin' Stevens are an essential part of the experience. But thanks so much for the offer!'

'What kind of experience though, man? Maybe I could just—' Nigel counters, edging towards the deck.

'MY EXPERIENCE! Pam says, her voice raised. She takes a moment to take a deep breath, composing herself. 'This is a Christmas experience arranged painstakingly by myself and my best friend and confidante Gilly. If you would like to host a mediation soul experience, you need to hire your own coach.' Pam looked away then, her eyes fixed steely ahead. Her legs, however, remained, acting as a last wall of defence against Nigel and his 'mediation experience'.

Nige shrugs and turns on his muddy heels, admitting defeat.

'Nigel, Nigel, mate, would you like a Malteser?' Asked Maggie

'I'm like vegan so, like, no thanks,' replied Nigel arrogantly.

Even Richie is shaking with laughter while watching Maggie, who's never one to give easily. She rummages around in the collection of carrier bags by her feet, hauls herself up, and follows Nigel back to his seat

'Here you are, my love, I was saving these, but you can have this,' said Maggie, stretching across my mum to proudly present Nigel with a single Ferrero Rocher on an outstretched palm. Even Jason was cracking up at his mother-in-law's Ho, Ho, Ho Matalan jumper that kept flashing more and more frantically each time her double FFs made contact with the side of my mum's cheek.

'Thanks, man, but they like contain animal products, so I'd rather, like, starve than eat it.'

'Are you sure? We are on our holibobs!'

Nigel tells Maggie he could list 'thousands of innocent animals killed or abused in order to make the chocolate in her palm.

Maggie scratched her chin and considered this.

'To be honest with you, I reckon someone's having you on. I mean, I very much doubt thousands of anything have been killed to make a Ferrero Rocher, Nige, mate. I mean, look, they're mainly nuts,' Maggie says, unwrapping the gold foil. Nigel starts to make retching noises.

'No?' Maggie says, shrugging and dropping the nutty ball into her mouth. 'Okay, no bother. Oh I know, what about a marshmallow Wagon Wheel or I might have a Walnut Whip knocking about in my bag?'

Three hours later

Currently sitting in a garage lay-by waiting for Gillian and Barnaby, as they're lost. Me, Jenna, Maggie and Nana are playing snog, marry or avoid, while Richie and Grandad take turns to say things like 'Don't worry, pal, we'll get you back on track' and 'What ya need to do is swing a left at the next turnoff and then 800 yards on your immediate right'. Down the phone is Gillian's husband (the one with the best sat nav in the world) while Pamela frets about us 'needing to get a move on' and refreshing the weather reports on her iPad. Mum and Nigel are dead to the world meditating (sleeping) after being the victims of a hate crime (being offered a chocolate).

Five hours after that…

It's snowing, and it's magical. But also freezing!

Just stopped at a big services to stretch our legs in Carlisle. Not too far away now. Something side-splittingly funny just happened. Jenna had decided to grab a sandwich and some rice cakes from the garage. After dithering about trying to decide if she wanted a chicken salad or a prawn wrap, we finally got to the counter, and the cashier, who had a bit of a Leonardo DiCaprio look about him (Think more *Wolf of Wall Street* than *Titanic* era), glanced up at Jenna as she dumped her items on the counter and said, 'Just wondering if you wanted to quickly grab a drink?'

Jenna flashed me a mock 'oh how embarrassing face' before replying quite smugly,

'Oh bless you, babes, that's so lovely, but I can't. I'm not from round here, plus…' Jenna purrs, holding up her ring hand. 'I am also married to that idiot over there.' Pointing to Jason, who's looking at a motorbike magazine.

'Umm no, sorry, but no what I meant was do you want to get a drink for your meal deal,' the server said, pointing down at the sandwich and SnackaJacks.

'Oh I knew exactly what he meant,' said Jenna, her cheeks still flushed as I attempted to send a voice note to the WhatsApp group, to tell them what had just happened. It took four attempts for me to be able to stop squealing enough to be able to get my words out.

Within minutes everyone had sent back laughing and crying emojis. Well apart from Val, who took nearly twenty and sent four aliens, an aeroplane and a tooth. She got a new phone for Christmas and she's finding the changeover from her Android to an iPhone tough.

Jenna and I sit opposite each other in the aisle seats, Jenna next to Jason and me next to Richie. Richie has his hand on the top of my thigh as we chat, the passing cars headlights illuminating the mountains and hamlets as they fly past us. Jenna starts to tell us about their honeymoon, again. From what shape the pools were, to how often the hotel changed the sheets.

'I sent Jase down to reception to complain. Once? Yeah, okay, I will let it slide. But not a second time. Not when it's my honeymoon on the line,' Jenna said, telling us about how the hotel had not replaced her (unused) soap on the flannel by the sink.

'You can take the mick all you like. But you'll be as under the thumb as I am soon, mate,' laughed Jason when Richie asked him what else Jenna had him complaining about while they were there.

'Hardly, mate, hardly, I am a free spirit, pal!'

Jason pointed out he was now half of a couple so wasn't free at all.

'What? Do me a favour! We barely know each other,' Richie replied, ha-ha-ha-ing.

I feel myself bristle. You know what it's like when you take something personally, but also know you're over reacting? Well that was me as I sat there telling myself not to act like a loon. He didn't mean it how it sounded. Despite me not saying a word, Jenna senses my mood and attempts to change the subject.

'Never thought of asking you to help, did I? When we was losing weight. We could have all come to you, couldn't we,' joked Jenna when she asked Richie if his fitness training business was still booming.

'Well not really, Jen, my courses are more for people with serious nutrition and fitness goals, than for people who just need to cut down on processed crap and get their arses moving.'

I glare at Richie then and said it before I even thought it in my own head. 'Excuse me? Who do you think you are? We make sure we hit our protein quota everyday, and we use My Fitness Pal. So don't say we don't have serious nutrition goals.' Jason and Richie laughed some more then, thinking I was joking. *Bite your tongue, Etta.*

By the time Jason had questioned how it was going to work long term between us, with Richie being based in Wales and me in St Ives and Richie had replied, 'Fuckin hell, slow down, I ain't ready for all that, pal!' Followed by 'And *if* we ever was it would be up to Etta to move to me cos, I have too much riding on Wales now. Too many ties.' I was fuming.

'Etta is in the same boat, to be fair,' Jenna countered, sensing I was about to snap.

'You can be a care assistant anywhere though, can't you? My business is established in the Brecon Beacons,' said Richie.

I can see Jenna is also raging now, so I shake my head in a 'don't even bother' fashion and Jenna flashes me the 'told you he was a prick eye roll'.

I then find myself thinking about what's just been said for a minute or two before getting to my feet and muttering something like 'nice to know'.

I heard Richie scoff something that sounded very much like 'grow up' as I stomped off down the aisle, plonking myself next to Maggie and Nana, who were tucking into a round of egg and bacon baps that Pamela had made at four this morning, and placed in a refrigerator box. Jenna followed and slings herself down next to me. 'Richie is such a tosser!' she declared, relaying what he had just said.

Maggie and Jenna's nana took it in turns to pat my hand, while saying things like 'He has always been the same' and 'A leopard doesn't change his spots!' in loud, accusing voices, while glaring in Richie's general direction.

'Do you know what you two remind me of, Etta, mate. You and Richie?' shouted Maggie over 'Fairy Tale of New York' after she gave a thumbs up to Pam who'd announced that there was only 'Ten more miles to destination!'

'Gavin and Stacey. Neither of them wanted to move either, but she wore him down in the end. We always do.'

CHAPTER 13

Midwinter Lodge, Tomatin, The Scottish Highlands

After nearly ten hours on the coach, we have arrived. The house and grounds are breathtakingly beautiful even in the dark. The snow, that has been falling here on and off for days, meant we practically crept along the winding single road as we approached the lodge. From the driveway you can clearly see the River Findhorn that snakes around the property. We were all taken aback when we set eyes on Midwinter Lodge; a grand, sprawling building, a former hunting lodge with about ten chimneys and a high-pitched slate roof, that sits elevated in the middle of a dense forest clearing.

'Oh, isn't this perfect? So festive!' Pam marvelled as she took in the forest, illuminated by the outside lighting dotted around the outbuildings and illuminating the grounds.

Gillian and Barnaby were not far behind us, crawling up the driveway. A fresh-faced woman crunched up the driveway directly after them, behind the wheel of an ancient Land Rover Defender.

'You arrived just in time,' said the woman as she held out a hand to Gillian.

'We're supposed to get another heavy fall tonight. Sorry, how rude of me. I'm Veronica, owner and host of this old place,' she said, gesturing to the imposing white stone building.

As Richie, Jason, Grandad and Maggie gave the bus driver a hand to unload, the rest of us followed Veronica, pausing as she clunked an oversized church key into the lock and stood aside, gesturing for us to make our way through the double oak doors.

'Oh Christ, it's like The Shining. We could all get murdered here. No one would hear us scream. Proper creepy!' Jenna had said sulkily as we went room to room, me pointing out all the original features and the tapestries. 'And I don't know why my nana and everyone keep banging on about how that bloody Veronica looks like Kate Winslet. I can't see it myself.'

For the record, the lodge isn't spooky, it's magnificent and Jenna definitely could see their host's likeness for Kate Winslet.

Anyway, let me take you on a little tour of Midwinter Lodge.

The main entrance doors open directly into a wood-panelled giant sitting room with a gallery double-height ceiling.

'The grand hall is my favourite room in the lodge,' Veronica had said, telling us to help ourselves to as many seasoned apple logs from the store as we needed during our stay, while gesturing to the crackling humongous open fire. The fire is what caught my attention first; the warmth making my cheeks instantly flush, followed by the heads of various stags' mounted to the wall above.

'This is going to be a very draining few days. So many souls, I'm already surrounded,' Nigel had muttered when his eyes had met the various stags. He said that he may need to sleep out in the woods to escape the demands of the dead, but would 'take some time to suss out the house's overall vibe first'.

The wide mahogany staircase leads up to a vast gallery hallway leading to the bedrooms; all of which have the customary red and blue tartan carpet and own open fire or wood burner. Four of the rooms are doubles, two with two double beds, and the last one has a set of bunk beds and a single. The rooms have en suites; a mixture of showers and roll-top baths, all have toilets with overhead cisterns. The double beds are mainly four-poster and the windows framed with drapes and thick valence curtains. I love how the customary red and blue tartan carpet clashes so unapologetically with the furnishings and upholstery; think Laura Ashley meets *Antiques Roadshow*, four-poster beds encased with silky drapes and thick valence curtains.

Back downstairs, the kitchen is surprisingly modern, with granite work surfaces and a Sub Zero fridge, both of which would look more at home in a plush London mansion, but there is a pillow-box red Aga and table off to the side with eighteen seats for, as Veronica called it, 'causal sups'.

The formal dining room is as grand as it gets. A dark wood table with at least twenty chairs tucked nearly underneath dominates the room. The walls, adorned in royal blue and gold wallpaper, are home to various framed oil paintings exclusively of hunting scenes/men on horses' and the odd ancestral portrait thrown in.

Above the stone fireplace is another mounted stag's head. There are a further three sitting rooms, a boot room, a pantry and a games room, where the children immediately shrug off their coats and sink into the bean bags in front of the wall-mounted plasma. Throughout the lodge there are tastefully decorated spruce trees and fresh foliage garlands. I notice the scent in the air is strangely familiar. Then I spot The White Company Candles burning in the corner of sitting rooms.

'Same as what you have at home,' I point out to Pam.

'They are, darling, I put them on the requests form,' replied Pam proudly.

'Right, first things first,' said Gillian, scooping up Captain. 'Shall we gather in the grand hall and allocate the bedrooms?' Gillian asks Pamela. We all do just that.

'Now, everyone, I don't know if any of you have noticed, but it has come to light that we only five bedrooms, not seven as per the website. But we do have an extra double bed in the front lead master suite,' Gillian informed us, armed with a clipboard and a serious expression.

After a bit of a discussion, we all, well, Pamela and Gillian, decided that the rooms would be as follows:

Pam, Grandad and Chloe in the room with two four-poster double beds. Open fire and river views.

Gillian and Barnaby in a four-poster double, with views and a wood burner.

Maggie and her husband (who has recently had some major hip issues so needs a decent bed.) Non-four-poster room, king-size bed and a wood burner and shower.

Nana and Jenna's boys' single room and bunk beds. With a large window that Nana definitely won't be 'having a quick puff' out of.

Jenna and Jason said they would be happy to sleep anywhere. I know Jenna was trying to let me and Richie have our own room and I appreciated it. Then my mum piped up after some rib nudging from Nigel.

'I feel I should make you all aware that Nigel is a medium and clairvoyant and therefore is finding the communal spaces here *very* challenging. He really needs a bedroom of his own, so that he can set up a crystal protection wall. Or I really wouldn't like to say what might happen.'

'Well, I suppose your father and I could take the settees in the games room,' Pam ventured. I could tell by her face that she was bitterly disappointed and furious. I had seen the way she had stroked the drapes in the thistle-papered bedroom.

I was about to rage, 'Don't be so stupid!' when Richie beat me to it. We hadn't even looked at each other since our little spat on the coach. I was expecting him to apologise, when we got to our room, but looks like that won't be happening now.

'I won't be having any of that, Pamela. You have gone to all this trouble arranging all this and, honestly, it's amazing. I am grateful to have been included, and you will sleep in a proper bed tonight. It would be an absolute liberty to even expect otherwise. And before you say anymore, let me just say, if you could see some of the places I've had to get my head down, you would know that a games room sofa is luxury for me. I'll take the sofa and I am sure Etta can crash in with Chloe.'

Pam beamed and nodded at me approvingly.

'Right, that's settled then. Let's get the kettle on, shall we?' said Grandad. And that was the end of that. Oh god, I hope Richie isn't going to dump me. If he does, it won't be my strop on the bus that did it, it will be the service station we stopped at the M73. No man should see any women under lighting that strong. Absolutely horrific. Men will put up with bad behaviour if you're beautiful. Bloody strip lights.

I'm writing this on night one of my romantic break, lying in a four-poster bed, a log burner crackling away, next to my daughter who's snoring and dribbling on my shoulder. While also listening to my grandad's snoring and Pam grinding her teeth. Meanwhile, Richie is sleeping downstairs on a four-seater sofa in the games room. The room is super cosy though, despite the snoring etc. I can hear the wind whooshing through the trees outside.

I wish I had stayed downstairs with Richie though. Maybe I should go back down with him, but he made it clear, I suppose, didn't he? Plus he should be the one to apologise. Or did I overreact?

Don't know what to think now.

Want to ask for Jenna's opinion, but her and Jason have got an early night as the boys wake up early and Jenna's nana had clarified that although she was willing to 'share a room with the little sods, come morning, they are your problems'. Jenna had said, 'Yeah, yeah, okay,' and pulled a face, but her nana caught it and said, 'I mean it, Jen. You won't see me up with the larks watching Power Rangers while listening to Maxwell list all the sodding Pokémon characters as I sit wishing myself dead; you're their mum, that's your job. This is my holiday as well, Jenna, mate.'

Decided to text the others in the Whatsapp group.

Etta 10:47pm

Hello, everyone, just to let you all know that we arrived safely. Jenna has had an early night. So have

I. Turns out there is only five bedrooms, not seven. Jenna and Jason are on a sofa bed and my mum guilt-tripped everyone into giving her and Nigel the last room. So Richie volunteered to sleep on a sofa! And said that I would be alright in with Chloe! (In the same room as Grandad and Pam!) And Richie and I had a bit of a tiff on the bus. He said we was nothing serious and that if we ever was, I would have to move to Wales. Oh and that his fit courses are not for people like me! Can you believe it! The lodge is great though, apart from all the dead stag heads all over the walls. How are you all? Nicky, are you glad your guests have gone?

I am not expecting a reply until morning, as everyone has to be up for work tomorrow. But Porsha does a few minutes after.

Porsha 10:49pm

Fuckin' hell, what a nightmare, babes. I have some funny news to cheer you up. Yana is making dinner tomorrow after work for Val, Nicky and me so can you and Jen try to FaceTime us then?

Said we would, then turned off my phone and decided to try and get some sleep. Don't want dark circles when I am dumped.

28th December, Midwinter Lodge, Tomatin, The Scottish Highlands

Felt nervous when I woke up this morning about seeing Richie, as I wasn't sure what to expect after him volunteering to sleep on a sofa. Felt ten times worse when I checked my phone and saw that he had sent me a text just past midnight that said simply:

Richie 00:00

Are you still up?

No kisses. But then Richie isn't really a kiss-adding person to messages anyway. Tried not to read too much into it. Then had a little think while I waited for Chloe to have a bath.

Fuck! I thought. I bet he wanted to dump me in private, oh gawd. But then when Chloe and I had come down for breakfast, Richie's face seemed to light up when he had looked round while adding an armful of logs to the fire in the wood burner in the kitchen and saw me.

'I fell asleep last night, didn't see your text until this morning,' I said apologetically as Chloe headed over to staggering amount of sausages, fried bacon, scrambled and poached eggs, laid out on trays next to the Aga.

'Gathered that,' Richie said laughing as Chloe skips past with her plate, the corgis and captain scampering along behind.

'You slept alright then? No ghosts I need to have a word with?'

'No, apparently Nigel and my mum have that covered. I'm sure they would have sent them all into the light by now,' I replied, rolling my eyes.

'I know it isn't really what we planned, but I felt bad for your grandad and Pam. We can't expect them to sleep on a sofa, that would be bang out of order.' My heart melted a bit then. He isn't going to pack me in or trying to keep away from me; he's just a really lovely and decent human being. Decided I had just taken what he said too much to heart yesterday. But still a question is niggling away at me; how could we ever work when he lives in Wales and I don't ever want to leave St Ives?'

I feel very lady of the manor today. All the shops always have such lovely cosy stuff; thick roll-neck, chunky knits and flannel pjs. But I always find that they are too warm for double-glazed homes and crammed pubs. I'm wearing black skinny jeans and a cream cashmere-mix jumper that was a present from all the girls for Christmas making the most of the cold weather. I am regretting my brown riding boots though, as although they look nicer than wellies, and match my coat and gloves, they are not the best choice in the slippery snow.

'The plan today is independent recreation before lunch, and then after a bracing group walk around the grounds at two this afternoon, Gillian and I will be heading off for a photoshoot, and so we have allocated more independently led activities such as reading, television or general conversing,' Pamela announced as Gillian continued.

'Supper will be at six, followed by adult drinks and board games at eight. Any questions?' Gillian added. We all shook our heads.

'Fuckin' hell, there's a secret library back here!' Jenna called, appearing from one of the sitting rooms. 'Etta, come and look! Its full of, like, books and it's got a ladder on wheels!'

By the time lunch was finished and cleared away, Gillian and Pamela had declared they would be 'cutting it too fine' to lead our first group walk, so asked Richie if he would take charge, while they got 'shoot ready'.

'I am not really into, like, snow, so I will just hang out here,' Jenna said after taking one look outside. George, Maggie's husband, also stayed behind as I've already mentioned he has some back and hip issues and didn't want to risk a fall.

'I was hoping to see your fluffy earmuffs,' Richie murmured down into my ear as we all plodded slowly next to the icy river.

'I don't have serious outdoor adventure goals you see, so thought I would leave them at home,' I reply, poking fun at his comments yesterday. Richie throws his head back and laughs, while reaching for my hand.

'Are you okay?' I call over to Maggie, who's just narrowly avoided walking into a tree, while crunching through the deep snow in moon boots.

'Yeah, sun was in my eyes, Etta, mate, all good,' She replies. Richie tells me he thinks that she can't see very well through her wraparound reflective shades, and because she's finding the Barbie pink ski-suit a tad restrictive.

This is later confirmed when Maxwell tugs on Maggie's arm and says, 'Nanny, why are you walking like the tin man from my book?'

Maggie calls him a 'cheeky little sod'.

'It is a bit tight on the tight size if I am being honest; I could have done with a size or two up, really. But they only had a size 24 in yellow and, well, I didn't want to look a tit.'

Grandad seems to enjoy listing all of the wildlife we should see while we are here. We all got excited for a moment, when Maggie had alerted us to a red squirrel in a Silver Birch, but it turned out just to be a normal squirrel that looked red due to her shades.

'I didn't mean nothin' by it, on the bus yesterday. I just like my private life to be just that, private. And we are still getting to know each other, ain't we? And all that I said about my business wasn't a dig at you, just meant that I couldn't up and leave,' Richie said, out of nowhere, as we walked through the walled vegetable garden and to the entrance of the woodland at the back of the house.

I got a bit shirty then and said, 'Well I also have commitments: my daughter, my family, my home, my friends. So don't worry, I wouldn't be in a rush to up and leave either.'

'I know,' said Richie. Neither of us said anything then for a little while. Because what was there to say?

'We would have to make it work. Somehow, because—' said Richie, cut short by Maggie screeching. Because what? Typical.

'Oh my life! I saw a pair of eyes! Evil beady ones. Something's stalking us! Richie! Richie, mate, Maxwell's just told me that Siri told him that there are wolves in these woods! Well I am tellin you now, if there are, then this ain't the place for us, love. I can't run from a pack of wolves. I ain't built to run!'

'We've only done a circuit round the grounds and river. We have the whole woods to explore yet!' Barnaby enthused, lifting his hiking pole in front of him. Maggie sucked her teeth and shook her head.

'Nah, I'm sorry, Barnaby, mate. I won't put the kids at risk. I think the best thing to do is turn back for the kids' safety. Who agrees we should, for the safety of the kids, get back to the lodge and gather round the fire with a nice hot chocolate, and maybe an extra little drop of Baileys for us adults?' I will admit my hand was one of the first to shoot up. 'I mean, we have been out for hours now, and although I was fully up for the five-mile route planned for us, well, now I've had that close encounter with the wolf pack, I think we really need to take it as a warning. What do we all think?'

Richie told Maggie that he was sure the 'evil beady eyes' she had seen were not wolves but was in fact just her eyes adjusting after she'd taken her snowboarding shades off after they'd caused her to trip over a log. Maggie chooses to ignore Richie's opinion and claps her hands together and shouts, 'Right! Come on then! Back to the house! You've all done so well. It's been treacherous out here and we have had a shock. That was a close call, that was with that wolf pack!'

We all started traipsing behind Maggie, our new self-appointed group leader. Who had wasted no time in shutting down Barnaby when he said that he 'very much doubted that a wolf pack would be less than two hundred feet from the house'.

'Well, opinion isn't fact, Barnaby mate,' Maggie had replied with her hands on her hips. 'And you'd be surprised how bold these wild and dangerous animals are these days. I mean, my neighbour's son's girlfriend's mum saw a badger by the trolley park outside Aldi last month. And a very aggressive-looking badger at that.'

'I had to wrestle a badger on Exmoor last summer. Come for my soul, he did,' said Nigel.

'See! Nasty little bastards,' Maggie said, while the rest of us howled with laughter.

When we got to the house, Maggie, looking very happy to be back, gave us one last speech as leader.

'Right, thank Christ for that! I managed to get you all back in one piece, and that's the main thing,' Maggie said as she turned to Maxwell and Chloe. 'And, kids, you've learned a lesson from today. We don't mess with wild wolves or badgers! You can tell your teachers that when you go back.'

'You heard it here first, Etta. Don't mess with wild wolves, and give those badgers a wide berth. Nasty little bastards they are,' Richie said, the sides of his mouth twitching as he helped pulled off wellies that seemed to have become fused to my feet.

I had just got the kids a snack and sat down in the library by the burner when I heard Jenna's hooting laughter and calls of 'Etta, come here!' I shouted back that nothing could drag me away from the steaming cup in my hand and the warmth from the fire.

'Your loss then, babes. It's Pam and Gillian. They think they're in a bloomin' Burberry photoshoot. Gillian's sitting up a tree holding dead birds!' Did I say nothing? I meant *almost nothing.*

What on earth are they up to?' I asked as Grandad shrugged his shoulders and we all crammed round the window for a better look.

'I know they mentioned something about a photo shoot, but I don't know where all those dogs have come from!' Grandad said.

'Don't know nothing about them, but I bet we're paying for them!' Barnaby said, shaking his head.

'Look, that bloke with the gun has just slung a string of dead birds over Pam's new blazer now!'

We all (bar Nige who said spectators were as bad as the savages who participated in blood sports) watched on, as the scene unfolded. I imagine it was a bit like witnessing a car crash; it's horrific, but you can't not look.

'Oh my god! That dog with the really waggy half tail just bit Gill's tit!' gasped Maggie.

'Christ sake, I do hope not!' Barnaby sighed. 'Seven grand those upgrades were, they're only a year old.' From what Pam and Gillian told us, in tight, clipped snippets of conversation when they arrived back covered in pigeon and pheasant guts, they had hoped to get some *Country life*-type photos, but hadn't foreseen, despite the owners' warnings, that the working dogs could be 'a bit on the bouncy side' when together and around fresh kill that it would go as it did. In the end Gillian had to offer up her new Fairfax and Favours handbag as a distraction to give them a window to escape from the scrum that the hounds had formed around them.

'Still, we got some fantastic frames our photographer said, so it will all be worth it in the end,' Gillian said. Pam, however, doesn't share her friend's optimism.

'My poor blazer! It has blood all over it. I am disgusted!' Nigel, who has reappeared sipping a cabbage tea, nods his head and tells Pam he 'completely gets it'.

'We all have the lightbulb moment where we realise what despicable human beings we are for what we have done and decide to make change. It is not too late!' Nigel preaches. Pam considers this for a minute, then agrees that she is disgusted with herself.

'I should have seen it coming. A hunter with armfuls of dead birds, me in my cream and strictly dry clean only, *new season* blazer. I am so ashamed of myself. I doubt even Johnson dry cleaners will be able to help me.'

Pam looks up to see Nigel shaking his head and muttering 'Unbelievable'.

'I know, darling, but even they can't work miracles. Let's keep our fingers crossed though,' Pam said placing a gut-smeared, comforting hand on Nigel's shoulder.

'Pam, mate, I know what you're going through, we have had our own trauma today. A near-death experience, in fact. Let's go and wipe those dog foot prints off your forehead, and I'll tell you all about it! Scared for our lives we was. And it was me that got us out of there! Soppy bollocks over there: 'Mr who dares wins' Maggie shouted, playfully pointing at an amused Richie 'Didn't know his arse from his elbow!'

As much as I would have loved to hear Maggie's account of our near-death experience, Jenna reminded me it was time to video call the girls.

'Shall we go upstairs where it's quieter?' I suggested to Jenna.

'Yeah, good idea, mate. JAAASSSEEE!' bellowed Jenna, loud enough to make my ears ring.

Jason appeared in the hall from the direction of the kitchen. I would say from the half-peeled potato in his hand, Gillian has roped him into preparing dinner.

'Jesus, Jenna, have you not got legs?' says Jason.

'Oh sorry! Jase, mate, sorry to drag you away from being your mum's slave. Shame you never help me like you do your mum, ain't it! Me and Etta are going upstairs to video call the other girls, and it's important, so can you watch the boys and Chloe?'

Jason nods as I thank him.

'I tell you what, I am about sick of his attitude!' Jenna moans as she climbs the stairs. 'Last night I was in bed and I said to him, "God, I'm so thirsty!" and he said "Are you?" and I said, "Yeah, I could well do with some of that M&S tropical juice in the fridge" and did he get up and get me one? Did he fuck! Four times I said it! In the end I had to go myself! I mean, what is his problem? Soon runs around for his mum though!'

I started giggling.

'It's not funny, mate, I tell you he don't look after me now we're married!' This made me giggle even more, because Jason will never stop running around after Jenna. Ever.

'Oh yeah and talking of my monster-in-law. You know I had to use the main bathroom and left all my bits out? Well I reckon Gillian is using my face cream! Last night it had all been moved, so this morning I laid a trap after I had a shower, put a vitamin tablet over the E on the pot and when I went up for a wee a minute ago it was on the L!' But I have come up with an idea to catch her out! She won't be able to deny it neither. She has shitloads of creams. It will be to spite me. Well, you wait, she's in for a shock!'

I asked Jenna what she meant and she started laughing and said, 'I won't ruin the surprise, but she won't be able to deny it, put it that way!'

That reminded me what I had heard Gillian say to Barnaby before we left. Jenna said that she didn't like Gillian, but if Jason's dad had 'done the dirty' then she felt a bit sorry for her.

'What she said at dinner last night makes sense as well, now you've told me that,' Jenna declared as we got to the bedroom I am sharing with Grandad, Pam and Chloe. I asked Jenna what she meant.

'Well, when we was all sitting down, I heard Gillian say, why is there a spare place setting next to me? When everyone is here.' To Pam, and then your grandad, who'd also heard what Gill had said, 'You've forgotten your husband, Barnaby is still in the kitchen getting the champagne.' Gill had chuckled when your grandad had told Barnaby that his wife had forgotten him, when he had appeared and taken his seat, but then I heard her snipe 'wishful thinking' under her breath.'

Well that doesn't sound good.

Val accepted our video call request, with a little wave.

'Hang on,' she said, propping her iPad on Yana's shiny work surface, and sitting down between Nicky and Porsha at the glass kitchen table.

Yana appeared on the screen, her London bus apron over red tartan pinafore dress, her face breaking into a warm grin as we swap waves.

'I finish the food, but I am also here and wearing the Scottish dress for you!' Yana says, giving us a twirl.

'So, what's the gossip then?' Jenna asks, readjusting her phone that had started to slide down the stack of pillows we'd stacked up at the bottom of my bed.

'Well there's a few pieces of news some fun, some less so.' Val replies, giving a little sideways glance to Nicky. 'Probably best we do the fun first.'

'Well,' begins Porsha, swishing her glossy jet-black hair extensions out of her face. 'My mate, you know Ryan, who works in the sun bed shop, Jen?'

Jenna nods.

'Love Ryan, so funny and always gives me an extra token.'

'So his boyfriend's sister was in town, yeah, on the day before Christmas Eve, and now this is deffo gospel, cos she is pregnant, seven months' gone she is, her boyfriend is the Chinese man who works in the bookies. So anyway, she woke up just before eleven at night and, well, fancied some southern fried chicken, and she has a little flat now, housing association, brand new with a balcony and only seventy-eight quid a week, right little touch, weren't it?' We all agree that it was.

'Bloody hell, Porsha, come on!' Jenna urges, yawning.

'Alight sorry, babes, so where was I? Oh yeah, so she wakes up craving chicken so off she waddles to Licken Chicken Good, and is waiting her five-piece bucket. Next thing she knows there's some like shouting coming from the flats opposite, not her block, the one right opposite Budgens. She hears a girl going mad, screamin' stuff like: "You complete and utter piece of shit!" And "What kind of dickhead thinks THAT is a gift for anyone, let alone a pregnant woman!' and then she said loads of men's trainers and proper shredded clothes come flying out the third-floor window. It all goes quiet for a minute, but then the front door opens, cause all those ones all have their own doors, and some girl in a really short bandage dress runs out, high heels in her hand, and she is followed by a man in a pair of boxers, who darts out and starts trying to pick up his shoes, he ain't even bothering with his clothes, cos they like fucked, and then the door slams behind him!'

You can tell Porsha is really enjoying building tension as she pauses with a knowing look on her face, green eyes sparkling, waiting for one of us to ask the question she's bursting to answer. So I indulge her.

'Who was it then?' Porsha's teeth are dazzling as she breaks into the biggest grin I've ever seen.

'So the man then spends the next ten minutes begging to be let in, but it's kicking out time and so the bird who locked him out probably can't hear him over all the laughter; pissheads mugging him off, making snapchats and that of him, cos he's like barefoot and wearing boxers in December. And guess who the man is? Robert, You know your ex Robert Ward!' Porsha clarifies in case I had forgotten.

'Fuckin' brilliant,' said Jenna.

'And there's more!' Porsha says.

'So my mate's sister keeps watching, while eating her chicken in the window seat of the takeaway, and for like a good fifteen minutes Rob's just outside, banging on the door shouting through the letterbox, things like: 'That's my fuckin flat! You can't lock me out my own fuckin' flat!' And she shouts back, 'Oh don't worry, dickhead, you can have ya shitty house back!'

But my mate's sister thinks that Robert thinks at this point, that the girl who's locked him out is blaggin' him and that he ain't gettin back in, cos he goes over to the chicken shop, in his boxers and a pair of trainers that smelled like bleach, and asked if they had a blanket and a phone he could borrow.'

Even Nicky, who's been very quiet, has had to remove her glasses now to wipe her eyes from the laughter. Porsha stops her own cackling and carries on.

'Fuckin birds are mental, ain't they!' Robert said. 'Even worse when they are up the duff! She's off her nut and locked me out, she has!' Robert announces to the whole shop and manages to get the owner to give him a phone. But he's g'tting flustered cos my mate's sister is also pregnant and mental and shit and glaring at Rob, so he can't remember anyone's numbers, so he is still standing by the counter tryin' to think of who to ring, when he spots his girlfriend coming out the flat, slamming the door behind her. She spots him and strides over, banging on the window of the takeaway and holds up a key to taunt him. So Rob rushes off to chase after her, still in his boxers.

'Give me my keys, you mental cow! You're off your fuckin' head!' he shouts at the girl as he follows her down the high street. The girl turns round and starts screamin' at him again,

'Off my head, am I? So YOU, the complete and utter wanker, decide to treat me to a threesome for Christmas with the local town bike WHILE I'M PREGNANT! And I'm the one off my head, am I? I'll show you off my head, you pisstaking dickhead!' And you'll never guess what she did? Only turned round and jangled the keys in her hand, and Rob goes to grab them but she's too fast, this is so fucking brilliant. 'Rob's there sayin', 'Don't you fuckin dare! That's my only set, my landlord ain't even got one and she's in Africa,' but the girl gives Robert the bird and posts the keys through Thornton's letterbox. And there's a big sign in the door that says: Closed till the New Year so, like, he can see the keys but he can't get them till, like, next year.

'Well someone has met their match!' Val says through laughter.

'I think Robert thinks he's Tom Hardy, but he is just a locked-out loser. We should call him Tom Hardly!' Yana tells us, chuckling at her own joke.

'Better she finds out what he is like now, I suppose,' I said. Everyone agrees. Not ideal, but it was inevitable.

'Hope she's okay,' said Val.

'Hopefully she is and hopefully Tom Hardly was outside just long enough for his dick to fall off!'' I said, agreeing.

'What a piss-taker! I mean who brings a random home to have a threesome with your unsuspecting pregnant girlfriend!' asked Jenna through more laughter. 'His self-belief is baffling!'

When the tittering subsides, I notice Nicky looks pale and tired.

'You okay, Nic?' I ask.

'Erm, well yes, I'm okay,' replies Nicky.

'Nicky is not okay, because Matt and family of Matt now say they go tomorrow and yesterday sister of Matt push Pinky the cat off Nicky's sofa and say you are bad cat and you must not get up again!' Yana tells us.

Me and Jenna look at each other, then back at the screen.

I wouldn't be having none of that shit, Nic! I mean, are you and Matt even okay now?' Poor Nicky looks like she may cry.

'It has been a very difficult few days and not what I was really expecting. Matt's been a little bit, umm distant,' says Nicky, looking to Val to take over the conversation. Val gives Nic's hand a comforting squeeze and tells us that its best to get them out of the house and then for Nicky to have a serious think about everything, including her relationship.

'Are they definitely going tomorrow then?' I asked, swapping a dubious look with Porsha and Yana.

'Yes, they said they'll be leaving tomorrow. There's been a gas leak on their road, you see, so they had to

~ 153 ~

delay leaving until it was back on,' Nicky tells me. But doesn't look much more convinced than Val, who's pursing her lips next to her.

We say our goodbyes, after they promise to update us tomorrow.

'Gas leak, my arse!' says Jenna when the call has ended. I tell ya there is something very wrong about this situation.'

I feel a bubble of anxiety rise in my stomach, because I know she's right. But, we can't do anything about it at the moment, and we know we can count on Porsha, Yana and Val to look out for Nic while we are here, so we decide to put it out of our minds and enjoy the rest of our time.

As we head back downstairs, we pass Maggie stomping past in a sports bra and high-waisted knickers.

'Very bloody misleading! I said to your mum, Etta, fancy your old man calling something a sound bath when there ain't no water involved! Took me ages to get in this bra as well. Could have been watching sodding *Home Alone* with everyone else. Bet all the Matchmakers will be gone now as well. Typical,' said Maggie, shaking her head.

CHAPTER 14

29th December, The Scottish Highlands

You'll never guess what happened today? Five unexpected guests turned up!

The day had been going normally, well as normal as it can be when you're sharing a house with Nigel and my mother.

'Right, I'll just grab a oak shake, man, then we can make a start on Diana's therapy session. She told me this morning she wishes to go first,' said Nigel after his morning makeshift Bikram yoga session, which he had created by running the shower on hot and shoving rolled-up towels under the door to stop any air flow to the bathroom. When Richie said he doubted that running a power shower on extra hot for nearly an hour would be that environmentally friendly, Nigel had said the water was a 'gift from the house for his services to his past occupants'. I didn't ask, because I really didn't want to know.

'This I have to fuckin' see,' Jenna whispered as my mum tottered off behind her not legal husband, enquiring if they would be using the dragon's blood or sage smudge sticks.

Today's events had started yesterday evening when Nigel had caught Pam on the hop after she had accepted a top up of her malbec with her filet mignon. The rest of us, including Gillian, had swapped 'what a load of old bollocks looks' as Nigel dived into his sales pitch of how he was 'a spiritual behavioural therapist' who had already gained confirmation from his spirit guide that he would be able to heal Diana so she could be a mother. When Maggie, who had polished off nearly four one-litre bottles of Smirnoff Ice and the spare portions of filet mignon that Pam and Gillian had cooked in case Nige or my mum 'changed their minds' about being vegans, she had had turned to my mum and said, 'Hilary, love, what's all this about how Nige will make Diana have pups?'

My mum's jaw had tightened. 'Nigel has the gift. He can speak to the animals.'

'Like Dr Dolittle?' Maggie asked, not looking convinced.

'I just want Diana and Charles to be happy, you see, darling. And to have puppies. She *needs* to be a mother.'

'I can make it happen, man, They both just need some therapy healing,' Nigel had drawled while I mouthed 'full of shit' to an already sniggering Richie.

It's true what they say about desperation; it makes you much more open-minded, but what they don't say is that it also makes you a bit thick. Which is the only reason I can offer by way of an explanation, as to why Pam, who is no one's fool, stood nodding in response to this madness and why we all piled into the grand hall to watch the spectacle unfold.

'It's your energy fields, man,' Nigel says with his eyes still closed and his nicotine-stained hands hoovering over a sleeping Corgi. 'I have just had a message. You need to remove the furniture at your house, and replace it all with vegan-friendly bamboo.' Pam looks uncertain. There is more chance of Pam removing me and replacing me with a vegan-friendly version than her getting rid of her new sofa and the Marks and Spencer hostess trolley.

But anyway, where was I? Oh yes, so Nigel convinced Pam to let him give the dogs therapy while she was tipsy on premium red wine and so we had now all gathered around waiting and watching. (And taking the piss.)

'But what are they saying about their relationship? I really want—' Pam is in full flow still as she is silenced by Nigel's grubby hand shooting up in a ssshh gesture.

'You alright there, Nige, mate?' asks Maggie as Nigel appears to be whispering and nodding into space.

'My old neighbour used to do that. Do you remember my old neighbour Colin, the one that always wore the beanie hat?' Jenna's nana asks Maggie.

'I remember him, he moved a while ago now, didn't he?' Maggie replied, her eyes till fixed on Nige.

'Didn't move as such. Got sectioned under the mental health act,' Nana says, frowning as Nigel slowly opens his eyes.

Maggie repeats her question. 'You alright, Nige, mate?'

'I was just consulting with Cheyenne warrior,' Nigel confirms.

'Cheyenne warrior? Who's that, babes?' asks Jenna, shooting me a smirk. She as loving this.

'That's Nigel's spirit guide,' says my mum.

'Well, one of them,' Nigel adds smugly. 'This is a very serious situation. But it's okay because Cheyenne warrior is here to help us. He is an extremely powerful Native American chief.'

'Although he is sending me messages as we speak. He is telling me that, Pamela, your aura isn't as open as it could be. So take a step back for me, please. I must cleanse and prepare my therapy space.

Pamela didn't need telling twice and sloped off to check on lunch. The rest of us, enjoying the entertainment, stayed put as Nigel laid out crystals around the still-sleeping dogs, and smudged the air with frankincense oil that, according to my mum, the air 'drank up due to the all the negative energies'. Nigel nodded knowingly, his dopey eyes fixing on me mainly, when she said that.

Nigel was all for removing the rugs and television, but Barnaby and Grandad, both concerned about their deposit, had to step in. When Nigel persisted, my grandad said, 'No can do, fella, I'm afraid.' With a look that said: 'Don't ask me again, I've already paid for yours and my drop-out daughter's lifestyle for the last thirteen months, I'm not having you fuck up my deposit as well.'

Nigel backed down then, and replied. 'No issues, man, I will sage them instead.'

Pam and Gillian rejoined us from the kitchen and were offering around honey-glazed cocktail sausages, just as Nigel announced he was about to 'spiritually imprint and bond with Diana'.

For once I heard Jenna agree with Gillian when she had sighed and said 'I have now heard it all.'

I had a little chuckle to myself as Mum assisted Nigel in plonking himself down next to now stirring Diana; the dog's lazy, bloodshot pupils eyeing them both up suspiciously as they ceremoniously began laying out a gold bowl, white feather and wooden stick.

'Now I will ask for complete silence while I begin working with Diana,' said Nigel as he signals to my mum, who begins chanting 'Om Shanti, Om Shanti'.

'Someone's ate all the fruitcake,' Jason announced to Richie, who chuckled in response.

'I must insist on silence!' my mum reminds us, glancing over at me and shaking her head slowly in a 'I am not amused' fashion.

'I've just had a message from another spirit guide, Sam the sailor, and he has explained that Diana is struggling to open to me due to your energy, so I need you all to accept the love and light I'm sending you and then send it on to Diana.' Oh dear god. Even Barnaby is gulping down his laughter now, while Jenna and Maggie are biting their knuckles trying to suppress theirs.

Nigel closes his eyes now, rubbing his wooden stick around the rim of his metal bowl, while making his way over to Diana.

'I'm not sure that's a good—' Pam is silenced once again by a confident (arrogant) Nigel who is now holding the humming bowl over Diana's head. She seems okay with it for a few seconds. Then, as Nigel re starts his chants of 'Om Shanti', Diana, true to character, turns on Nigel without warning with the speed of a quarter horse, jumping up at his face like a snake attacking its prey. Everyone, Nigel included, gasps as a snarling Diana takes a meaningful lunge at Nigel's forearm.

'Aaaaaarrggggh!' screeched Nigel. Who takes a few seconds to regain his composure.

'Keep calm, gang. Diana is doing as I instructed and releasing her valve of negative emotions from deep within before she accepts my love, light and guidance,' says Nigel.

Oh fuck off.

Nigel selects a large white feather and holds it up in front of him. He looks a bit like the monkey on *The Lion King* when he presents baby Simba to the animal kingdom.

I am half expecting a pan pipe remix of 'The Circle Of Life', when Nigel announces: 'I shall now use this powerful feather blessed by the elders of my Native American Indian tribe to imprint with Diana.'

'Nigel, Nigel, darling, thank you, but I think we should leave it here. It's, it's just that the dogs can't really be trusted around feathers, well anything with fur really, not after the misunderstanding with number seven's ferret, but especially feathers, because they had a toy once with a feather on it and—' For the third time Pam is cut short by Nigel waving her concerns away with a dismissive shrug.

'This is no ordinary feather, man, this feather has been selected and cleansed by some pretty powerful spirit guides. Cheyenne warrior was a village chief, warrior and elder,' said Nigel.

'Not to be confused with the reasonably priced four by four,' Jason whispered to a now-proper- shoulders-shaking-as-he-is-laughing-so-hard Richie.

'It's just that Diana, in particular, really doesn't like feathers—' Again Pam is cut short, this time by Maggie, who doesn't want the show shut down before the main act.

~ 160 ~

'Pam, mate, I'm sure it's fine. Nigel is not only a medium and animal therapist, he is also a reiki master. You have a certificate and everything, don't you, Nigel?'

Nigel nodded and replied simply, 'Yes, Maggie, yes I do.' Then the smug fucker says that he will start with Diana as she is 'more open and ready to receive healing'.

'Well, if you're sure, Nigel, but be alert, as she's liable to turn on you,' warns Pam, shooting my Grandad a look of concern.

The next few moments can only be described as carnage, but incredibly funny carnage.

Diana, it seemed, as Pam had feared, did not give one single shit that Nigel was a Reiki master, or that as he had announced to her and the whole room that he was approaching Diana with 'love and the channelled support of Cheyenne warrior'. Diana did, however, give lots of shits when Nigel leaned right down by her face and attempted to wipe her nose with the spirit guide selected and blessed feather. Talking on spirit guides, after what I have just witnessed, I can only presume that Mr Warrior got confused and channelled his hunting/ battle vibes rather than his calm village elder ones to Diana.

Who knows? But what I do know is; by the time Grandad managed to prise Diana's locked jaw from Nigel's chin, leaving his own claret smeared all over his face, I couldn't helping thinking that Nigel resembled an Indian warrior chief himself.

'Well we don't need to be able to speak to the animals to know Diana just told him to stick his feather up his arse and go fuck himself, do we?' Jenna's nana asked us as she hooted so much she needed two goes on her blue asthma puffer.

'Maybe Diana was more tuned in to the negative energy than you thought?' Mum offered while applying witch hazel to Nigel's war wounds.

Clearly not wanting to lose face, Nigel replied, 'Yes, Diana is indeed a very troubled soul. She just told me a story that was the cause of her losing control of her emotions. It all stems from a past life, you see. None of the aggression you just witnessed was for me! Diana has nothing but love for me. I reminded her of her enslaver when she was an Egyptian maid. The way she was treated! She murdered him you see, her enslaver, when she could take no more. With a few more sessions we will get there. She's made so much progress today, Pam!'

Nigel called out, 'Diana has just disclosed that she's ready to be a mother, so that's big progress!'

Pam nodded and agreed. 'Yes, great news.' In the most unconvincing, upbeat voice I've ever heard.

'Plus she's actually sending me messages of remorse and begging for forgiveness as we speak. What we mustn't do is hold it against her. None of this is Diana's fault. I mean, just look at her, that's a dog in turmoil, man,' Nigel said, gesturing to the other side of the room.

We all shifted our eyes over to Diana, who was sitting on Pam's lap, wrapped in her special 'calm down, calm down' blanket, chewing away on the M&S topside of beef slices that Grandad had been instructed to fetch her 'for the shock'.

'She doesn't look like a dog in turmoil to me,' Jenna said. 'That bloke is like loco, like really proper mental, ain't he?'

'Yes, Jenna. Yes he is,' I say, imitating Nigel's slow hippy drawl.

Porsha called us this evening.

'Hiya, babes, so I need some help. I am thinking we should get hold of Rupert Campbell-Black and the rest of the posse, to come and meet our book club. Maybe not that Janey, cos well once a slut, always a slut, and I don't want anyone coming between Reg and Margaret, and I've seen the way Reg raises his eyebrows when the audiobook mentions Janey. What do you think? How would we find them? I've searched all their names on Insta and can't find none of them.'

Spent the next ten minutes explaining that a novel means fictional, then a further five explaining what fictional meant.

'So they ain't like real people?' Porsha asked me, her voice sounding as deflated as a child learning the truth about the tooth fairy. 'I can't believe it, they sounded so real.'

'Yeah, babes, it's cos a writer has made them up and it's like her job.' Explained Jenna. I then suggest we write to Jilly Cooper and see if she would visit.

'Nah, if Rupert won't be coming, don't bother,' Porsha said, not even trying to hide her disappointment.

'This is worse than when I had to prove dragons were not extinct because they didn't ever exist,' Jenna laughs as Porsha rolls her eyes.

'Has Matt and his freeloading family gone? No one has answered my Whatsapp,' I said

'Nic said not to bother you two with it, but, no, they ain't yet. Think Val and Yana are going round there later.'

I wonder what the reason is this time. Power cut? Or a flood, maybe?

CHAPTER 15

30th December, Midwinter Lodge, Tomatin, The Scottish Highlands

Nigel set the tone nicely at breakfast, curtesy of a YouTube video entitled 'UK slaughterhouse secret recording 2009' and the flat-screen television in the kitchen.

'What is the meaning of this!' demanded Gillian, who had just forked a dainty portion of scrambled eggs and crispy smoked bacon into her coal lipstick-lined mouth.

Nigel said it was time for 'extreme action' and that we all had a 'responsibility to know what happens to the animals put to a gruesome death to feed our deprived faces'.

Pamela attempted to turn off the video, but after faffing around with the remote and only managing to turn up the volume, Richie leaned over and pulled out the plug.

'You need to tone down the combative veganism, pal,' he said as Nigel lunged towards the plug, but thought better of it when Maggie gave him one of her 'come on then, let's be having you' glares while biting into her sixth sausage of the morning.

'You eat processed meat, therefore need to be educated,' whined Nigel.

'Processed meat? How dare you! You would do well to know that is Daylesford and therefore both organic and free-range!' ranted an outraged Gillian.

'Oh god, is it? I wish you'd said,' said Maggie, turning her nose up at remnants of the bacon, eggs, sausages, hash browns and black pudding on her plate.

'I don't trust free-range meat, mate. I mean, how can you? You don't know where it's been?' Jenna's nana agreed.

'I'm the same with fruit and veg. If it ain't from one of the nine supermarkets and in a plastic bag, I ain't buying it!'

Grandad asked Nana which shops she considered the 'big nine'.

'Tesco, Sainsburys, Lidl, Aldi, Iceland, Spar, Nisa, Asda and Waitrose, but you have to watch them, they try and sell the free-range as well,' Jenna's nana told my grandad.

Nigel said no more as he rustled up a carrot, cumin and celery shake, then helping himself to Gillian's new Thermos flask, much to Jenna's delight and Gillian's horror.

'Will you be joining us for a ramble this morning?' Barnaby asked my Mum. Mum said that her and Nigel were being called away to 'an urgent matter' (dark entity causing havoc in a three-bedroom semi an hour's drive from here) and that the lift would be arriving shortly and they wouldn't be back late this evening. We all perked up then thinking that we wouldn't have to endure any more lectures about what terrible humans we were, but just as we were layering up, pulling on wellies and telling the kids that, 'Yes, they really did need to wear the hat and, yes, also the gloves', Nigel appeared, declaring that he would in fact have time, after all, to join us in a 'barefoot connection with nature'. Fantastic.

We only ended up walking around the estate for about half an hour, because without sounding like a knob stating the obvious, it was SO cold! Like bitter cold. It really is breathtakingly beautiful though. Like a painting. Too perfect to be true. Jenna had stayed at the lodge with her youngest, because it really was freezing, and also because she wanted to watch *Real Housewives of Beverly Hills*. I have to say I was surprised when my mum and Nigel joined us carrying carved sticks and smocks made out of something that looked very much like some kind of animal hide, given Nigel made noises like he was about to vom when I plonked my leather gloves down next to him yesterday.

'I thought you were vegan?' commented Gillian, beating me to it, obviously still brooding after Daylesford gate this morning.

'We are,' said my mum, looking a bit shifty.

'If you are referring to the skin, they were gifted to us from a very powerful American Indian chief as part of an energy-swapping ceremony. It would been a huge disrespect to my spirit guide to have refused them,' replied Nigel, reaching for my mum's hand. I then asked, with more than a hint of sarcasm, if this was the same Indian chief that supported him in getting attacked by a severely obese Corgi. I couldn't help myself. Pamela and Grandad both gave me the 'No more of that' look, but Pam's look was probably because I had referenced Diana's even greater weight gain in the last month.

'You didn't tell me you had been to A-mer-ric-ca, Hilary!' my grandad enthused, changing the subject. The way he said America like it was another planet made me chuckle. Mum then said she hadn't told him, because she hadn't been.

'Oh I see,' said Grandad, grabbing hold of Pamela as she let out a shriek, her Hunter welly slipping on a slippy strip of icy path.

'How did you get your special energy jackets, then?' Grandad asked enthusiastically. I can't even look at Richie. His hand, shaking in mine, tells me that he is trying to surpass his amusement as much as I am.

'An Indian free spirit event in Gloucester,' said Mum, primly.

'Oh, how interesting! Is there a large Native American Indian community in Gloucester?' Grandad persisted.

'No,' came the response.

Like trying to get blood out of a stone comes to mind. Bless Grandad though. He has always been so keen to engage everyone in conversation and make them feel welcome. I had a little smile to myself on the way up here, listening to snippets of his conversations.

'SBS then, Richie? Cor, bet you have some stories, ay?' 'Oh lucky you, Maggie! I have seen those package holiday adverts on the television.' 'Oh what's that you're playing, boys? Oh a Nintendo. Very posh.'

Pam and Gillian had organised a whiskey tour for today. Maggie and Jenna's nana hadn't needed a lot of persuasion and had eagerly got their coats on upon the confirmation of 'yes there will be free samples', Maggie then telling her husband George to wear something with pockets. Grandad isn't really a drinker, but had also agreed to tag along to keep Barnaby, Gillian's husband, company.

The distillery had arrived in a mini painted bright red with 'The Whiskey Chasers on tour!' embossed down the side. Pam had invited (insisted that) all of us come and pose for photos outside by the bus with shot glasses of apple juice in hand, before they left.

Jenna and Jason, who wasn't understandably that keen to spend an hour and a half in a minibus each way, had offered to stay behind and look after the dogs and kids.

Jenna suggested that Richie and I should make the most of it and go off on our own for a few hours. Chloe, happily setting up the just dance mat in the games room for her and Jenna to have a rematch, said she didn't mind and that Jason had also planned a game of hide 'n' seek in the house after the video games.

Jenna rolled her eyes in a 'fuck sake way', agreeing that she would play 'for the sake of the kids', but then turned to Jason and said, 'Nice one, mate, promising kids things. I tell you what, Jase, the first time I hear even a noise that sounds even remotely like a clap, I'm out! And no one is to get into a wardrobe!' Jenna had warned.

'Oh stop being a spoilsport,' Jason said, ruffling Jenna's hair.

'I've seen *The Conjuring*, I know how these things go down, and it won't be you tied to a chair having holy water slung in ya face pal, no. It will be muggins here!' replied Jenna, pointing at herself dramatically.

Gillian had reluctantly let Richie borrow their Land Rover in order to drive the two miles each way to the local pub, where he was taking me for lunch. After quite an extensive 'chat'.

'This isn't your average car, Richard. Please remember that. You are in sole charge of a powerful and deadly weapon. It is a responsibility not to be taken lightly,' Gillian had reminded Richie.

Richie assured her he was good at handling powerful, deadly weapons, would utilise his eight years' SBS experience, and his twenty years' driving experience to handle the Land Rover carefully. And, yes, he promised not to park too close to kerbs.

'Twenty years, you say?' Gillian asked, looking at Richie dubiously, but you're only what?'

'Thirty-five, yeah, he is,' Maggie joined in. 'Little sod was fourteen when he started to pinch his mum's car, little joy rides up to Wimpy, sometimes got as far as Skegness, once even got as far as London, didn't ya?' Maggie chuckles ruffling Richie's hair before clocking panic spreading over Gillian's face.

'All in the past now though, got selected by Elite Boat Service he did, so your motor's in safe hands.' Maggie added.

I felt a bit like Cameron Diaz in *The Holiday* when Jude Law drives her along the lanes of the glorious Cotswolds on their first date. Had a bit of a moment. Looked over at Richie and smiled as he lifted one his, as Yana calls them, 'shovel-like hands' off of the steering wheel, to gently squeeze the inside of my thigh. His navy Stone Island jacket that his whole family had presented him with, proudly explaining that they had all chipped in to get him for Christmas, straining slightly over his broad shoulders, as he could have really have done with an XXXL, but didn't want to seem ungrateful.

'Richard, you are not taking your pledge to me seriously! This is my 22 plate Landie on the line here! Both hands on the wheel!' I joked in high-pitched, nasal voice.

The pub, a Tudor building with a steep, bumpy car park and some long since dead hanging baskets being blowed about violently in the fierce wind looks like it needs a refurb. Inside is worse. Stained carpets, mismatched wobbly chairs, yesterday's fire remnants in a pile at the side of the grate. But it's warm, cosy and welcoming.

'Don't say I don't know how to treat you,' Richie says, pulling out my chair and handing me a laminated menu he grabbed from the bar. I notice he keeps the one with gravy stains on back for himself.

'So what will it be? Scampi and chips, pie and chips, cheese and chips or, steak and, you guessed it, chips!' said Richie, scanning the limited menu and giving me a playful glance.

I have been a little lapse on calorie counting, vowing myself these few days off, so go with the cheesy chips. Not to sound like Pam, but I wasn't confident in the chef's ability to not give me food poisoning if I chose meat. And I am not being a snob, but it was a two-star hygiene-rated premises. Which means the chef didn't prepare the food on the floor.

Richie says he has a stomach of steel and is going with the steak, excusing himself to go up to order our drinks and food.

He is at the bar a bit longer than anticipated after the bar staff, clocking his accent and offering a phrase we had heard increasingly as we had got further up north, 'You're a long way from home, where are ye from?'

I didn't mean to look as Richie's phone beeped. I had just glanced on autopilot, just a natural reaction. Then I saw it.

The name Nicole illuminated on his screen next to a photo of a girl; she looked a bit like a model. Not a real one, one of those ones you see on Instagram selling BoomBod.

It was a Whatsapp notification. I creaked my neck to try and catch what the message said, feeling my chest tighten. I can only read part of the screen, but it reads:

Sorry hun missed ur call lst nite. Can do the 2nd babe. NP cu then. Xx.

Can do the second? Sorry I missed your call? Oh great, I think, as my heart starts to pound and my ears and cheeks burn. I haven't felt like this since I was wearing a pink jumpsuit and got called Percy Pig in a crowded pub.

Who the fuck is Nicole? I rage in my own head, as Richie comes back with our drinks. Don't act like a psycho, Etta. Just keep your shit together, it may be nothing, I tell myself, while already deciding it definitely is something.

I watch Richie's expression carefully when I say causally that he got a message while he was at the bar.

'It's not Jenna telling us she can't cope already, is it?' I ask jokily while inwardly I'm screaming.

'Nah, just work, nothing important,' Richie replies still looking down at his phone. I see him switch it to silent, before placing it back on the sticky table top.

I say nothing, but think a lot. Mainly along the lines of: Who is Nicole, tell me now, you fucker!

If Richie notices I am struggling to carry on as normal, he doesn't let on. I almost ask him outright, but if it is nothing, then I know I will look nosey and weird. But why lie about it?

Richie still seems utterly oblivious to my frosty undertones as my mind races while trying to keep up with his chatter about plans for his business in the forthcoming year.

'Why Wales, though?' I asked.

'Did a lot of my training in the Beacons, well, there and Poole. Jim, my pal, found the place cheap. Perfect conditions for what we do.' I watch his sapphire-blue eyes light up as he then tells me some of the other places he has been while in the SBS.

I decline dessert (bread and butter pudding with Bird's custard, or Eve's pudding and Bird's custard). Richie orders one of each and declares it 'blindin', thanks' when the waitress, a young, slim girl in her early twenties, slinks over to ask 'if everything was okay with your meal'. Did he wink at her? I think to myself. As I look up from my phone, did I hear her give a girlish giggle as she walks back to the bar with a flick of her ponytail. Or am I now seeing things that aren't there?

On the way back to the house, Richie asks me about the access course I am starting in January, the course I need to pass to be accepted to university. I try to put the text I've seen out of my mind as I explain what it is and what I will need to do after. But I just can't stop thinking about it.

Jenna can tell by my face that I am not okay, before I have even unwound my scarf from my neck. She mouths, 'You alright?', narrowing her eyes at me. I shake my head.

~ 173 ~

'Oh, Etta, babes!' Jenna says loudly enough for Jason and Richie, who are watching the kids play poker for Haribo (a skill learned curtesy of Jenna's nana). 'Can you come and help me do that hair thing now?'

'What's happened, mate?' Jenna asks as she closes the door to the main bathroom. I tell her about the text and everything that came after.

'*That shitbag*. This better not be anything cos if it is, well… I will fuck him right up. What was her name again? The little cow that's texting him?' Jenna demands, picking up her mobile.

'Nicole.'

'Right, I'm on it. We will get to the bottom of it.' I ask Jenna if she thinks I should just ask him.

'Urgh, definitely no. Have I taught you nothing, babes? You can't ask them before you already know. Cos once they know that you know, but you can't prove what you know, you're fucked cos you give them the chance to spin you a line, and cover their tracks. They're all fuckin' liars, mate, some less than others, but they're all the same really. So you need to come with receipts, then we give them the rope and watch them hang themselves. But it might be nothin', so don't get yourself in a state.'

I could tell by Jenna's tone that, despite her reassurance, she thinks it is definitely something, just like I do.

I knew it was too good to be true. Who has a photo of themselves in a bikini as their WhatsApp photo? Fucking narcissist.

Jenna has said she will try and find out who the woman is by looking at Richie's very limited social media.

'If we draw a blank I will have Jason find out.' When I ask if Jason would even do that because Richie and him are friends, Jenna rolled her eyes and said, 'Yeah, but I'm Jase's wife, mate, so he will do what I ask him to. He knows where his bread's buttered, babes, don't worry about that.'

We gave Val a ring when we're back downstairs, to check that Nicky's visitors have left.

'Hello, shall we switch to video, all the girls are here,' Val says. Jenna sends the request to swap to video screen and we both sit cross-legged on the floor by the wood burner in the library.

'That is one beautiful room,' whistles Val, like Grandad does when someone tells him something he finds impressive. All the girls crowd into the camera, taking in the background of the library; floor-to-ceiling books and parquet flooring, framed by the bay window, is an impressive sight, I have to admit.

'Right,' says Val, her tone serious and regretful. As we all expected, Nicky's guests are still very much in situ. We are just discussing what to do next.'

Porsha leans into the camera and waves. 'I have said I can have my Mikey go round and chuck 'em out with a few of his mates; one of them has got this staffie that—'

'I've said it's probably best we try to deal with it without violence,' Val says. 'But we will bear it in mind.'

I ask Nicky, who's sitting picking at her nail polish on Val's lounge sofa, what Matt and his family have said by way of an explanation of them still not leaving.

'Well… They haven't said anything, they just are still there. I asked Matt this morning, and he got incredibly grumpy and said that they would be going tomorrow afternoon.'

'I go to pick up Nicky for the aerobics and Matt and Mum of Matt say, "What you want? Who is you at the door?" Through letterbox, like they hide from someone. I say this is Yana, I am friend of Nicky, and they open the door and say you are too early, she is still at the Aldi and slam the door in my face! I do not like these people! They are very rude. And the mother of Matt, she was wearing the new jumper of Nicky!' Yana tells us.

Jenna asks Nicky why Matt's mum was wearing her new clothes.

'She helped herself,' said Nicky, feebly. I asked her if bedroom arrangements had changed at all. 'Sadly not,' Nicky confirmed.

'I personally think, mate, it's like well weird that Matt ain't sleepin' with you cos you're like well bangin', babes,' Porsha said as Nicky blushes and says, 'Thank you, I appreciate that.'

'Plus,' continues Porsha, 'Why is Matt's sister sleeping on the sofa in the same lounge as Matt, her brother? When Nicky said her spare room has like two double beds in it. Would be better for the sister to share with their mum, wouldn't it?' We all agree it is strange.

'See, that's the whole other thing. It makes me wonder what we discussed before. Are they who they say they are? Is Matt there because he wants to be in a relationship with Nicky? Or, and I am sorry to say this, Nicky, is he there for another reason?' says Val.

Nicky looks like she's about to start sobbing, but pulls it together and admits that Matt has barely uttered two words to her since he's been there.

'When he does speak to me, it's mainly to ask if I can pick him up some more cigarettes from the shop, or for the code for the Sky box office. That kind of thing.'

'Hold up,' Jenna said, frowning, her palm raised to the screen. 'Who are the fags for? Matt told you he didn't smoke, didn't he?'

'Yes, he did. But he does smoke, and so do all the rest of them,' Nicky confirms.

'What about if Val, Porsha and Yana go to yours with you now, and tell them to leave?' I ask, sensing Nicky's anxiety.

Nicky dithers about for a minute or two, saying that she doesn't want to have a confrontation, but finally agrees to let us help her word a text to Matthew to send now, asking him to leave.

After rejecting Jenna's suggestion of: 'Get you, your freeloading family and all your fucking shit out of my fucking house by the time I get home from work tonight or else!'

Nic settles on:

Matt, this is not working between us. You have said three times you will be leaving since you invited yourself and your family into my home, yet you remain in my house. I have no choice therefore but to now INSIST that you, your family and all of your possessions, are to be out of my property by tomorrow midday. I will be calling by after work to collect my cats with Val, and we shall be returning tomorrow and expect you all gone. Nicky

I had suggest that Nicky stay with one of the others this evening, as I know she is so kind-hearted and would feel uncomfortable returning home tomorrow.

'And if they do not leave by tomorrow?' Yana asks

'Then we investigate the fuckers and make them!' Jenna says. 'No one takes the piss outta my mate.'

'Couldn't agree more,' said Val.

'Right, thank you, ladies. That's that sorted for now. Tell me, how're things your end?' Nicky asked, clearly wanting to think about something other than three virtual strangers taking over her home for a few moments.

'Good, the house is amazing, and it's so very nice up here, but cold!' I giggle.

'Etta has a problem though, don't ya, mate,' Jenna said before launching into a full account of my pub date with Richie.

'Now, I may be going senile in my old age,' Val says, 'But before you start the latest MI5 investigation, could you not just, in fact, ask him, Etta? Explain you saw the message and ask who she is? It could save a lot of upset?'

'Blimey, Val, you don't ask men questions you don't already know the answers to!' Says Porsha.

'Exactly, babes!' said Jenna, nodding in agreement.

'I think maybe I also like to know, before I ask Simon the question, if I think he being the sneaky,' agrees Yana.

I ask Nicky what she thinks.

'Gosh, don't ask me, I have a man and his entire family sitting in my lounge watching re-runs of *Jonathan Creek* and eating me out of house and home. And I only accepted an invitation to dinner. I am last person you should ask!' laughs Nicky. I don't know if it's the release of the tension she's kept bottled up, or the dire situation she's in ringing home to her, but once Nic starts laughing she can't seem to stop. Pretty soon we are all howling.

'Well, whatever happens, at least we have each other, hey?' Jenna says.

'I watch a programme the other day and they say the good quote. Real friend can't half in. You need to be there when they call to party at 2am as well as at nice party at 6pm,' Yana says, nodding her head.

'Blindin quote that, where did you hear it?' Porsha asks.

'*The Mob Wives*,' Yana replies. ITV2. Very, very good. Lots of drama, very much drama. I also love the clothes.'

'That's what I mean. If you need me to bally up and go round yours, Nicky, mate, and drag them out for ya, then I'm down for that, cos that's what real friends do.' Porsha agrees with Jenna and promises Nicky that she's also more than down to back her 'all the way'.

Val says she is also willing, but would rather not have to physically assault anyone, as her knee still 'has been better' but, 'if push comes to shove' she also would not back down either.

Just as it was getting very *Sopranos*, I heard Pamela screeching like I've never heard her before.

'Come quickly, Diana is pregnant and also in labour now!'

'Diana's having pups?' I say, swapping confused glances with Jenna as we say our goodbyes and gallop down the stairs to see what all the fuss is about.

Jenna's nana confirms Diana is 'deffo up the duff and about to pop' and tells us she needs some scissors, a boiled kettle and get a load of towels 'sharpish'. Jenna asks her nana if she should call a vet.

'A vet?' huffs Nana. 'I've seen every series of *Call The Midwife*, twice. I don't need no vet!'

Jenna sets off in search of her make-up bag to retrieve some nail scissors.

'Fuckin' hell, that was fast!' Maggie says as she flicks the kettle on and I place a pile of towels above the Aga to warm them. 'I mean Nigel only done his spell earlier today. I *must* speak to him later myself about the eight stone I've been meaning to shift.'

I couldn't tell you what went down in that room, well I have a child of my own, so could tell you, but it wouldn't make for good reading. Once was bad enough. Imagine having five of them after another. Ouch.

Jenna and I made ourselves useful, we didn't abandon ship completely, we took it in turns in piling Pam with double brandies, while Gillian consoled her in sympathetic tones while saying things like 'you weren't to know, you mustn't blame yourself' and 'dogs have a way of hiding things' as though Diana was a teenager and Pam was her frantic with worry mother, beating herself up, muttering things like 'I should have seen the signs!' After just discovering her privately educated daughter is addicted to heroin.

Still, all's well that ends well. The puppies arrived safely, no harm done. And Pam, who seemed a lot more chill after Maggie had given her half of an unknown pill to 'Calm her down a bit' suggested we have an Indian takeaway to celebrate. Ritchie and Jason had to travel half an hour each way to collect it though, so it was a bit cold when they arrived back with it, but we warmed it up in the Aga.

'So useful these Agas; first it warmed the towels for Diana's puppies! Then it warmed a meal for sixteen. I think I would like one of these!' Pam said to my grandad as she floated in for more napkins.

'Might ask Maggie for the other half what she had,' I said to my grandad, who laughed and shook his head.

'To Charles and Diana and their puppies!' shouted Barnaby, raising his glass as we all tucked in around the dining room table.

'To our Christmas miracles!' Pam enthused, clinking her glass with Gillian.

The puppies were certainly a miracles. Bright-orange, fluffy miracles. Which makes me wonder just how much Charles has had to do with these certain 'five gifts from god' as Pam now keeps referring to them as.

'Don't take a genius to work out, does it?' said Jenna, topping up her champagne. And shovelling more beef madras from the silver foil tray and onto her plate and raising her eyebrows as Gillian's Pomeranian darts past out of the room, closely followed by Gillian squawking,

'Captain James! give Mummy that rib bone! Listen to Mummy right now, you naughty boy!'

Oh well, as Val said, ignorance is bliss, until it isn't.

When the kids went to bed, I was trying to pluck up the courage to come out and ask Richie, but there just wasn't a right moment. Jenna also couldn't find anyone called Nicole on his social media pages. Decided to put it out of my mind for this evening.

It was actually a brilliant night. Barnaby had excused himself and said he was going to have an early night and offered to listen out for the kids so Jenna and I could relax.

We all settled in the games room, Maggie put her favourite songs playlist on, which Gillian and Pamela appreciated as it was very heavy on the Lionel Richie and Diana Ross.

Although Gillian did have a bit of a moan at about two am, when she was woken up by Jason and Richie, who'd been rolling around the dining-room floor pretending to be ninjas.

'*What* do you think you are doing?' she had scolded them while standing in her floor-length nightie.

'Sorry, sorry, Mum,' slurred Jason, while choosing the exact same moment to spoon a heaped dessertspoon of left over lamb korma, still on the table from dinner as Pam had said daringly, six hours previously,

'Let's go mad, Gilly, darling, and leave it all tonight, we can deal with it tomorrow. Let's just close the doors and say, that can wait until the morning!'

I let out a large laugh as I watched Jason concentrate on the spoon, but still somehow manages to miss his mouth completely and pour the stone cold korma all over his nose and cheek.

'*What on earth* do you think you are doing?' Gillian demanded while Richie, Jenna and I were doubled up with laughter.

'That *is not* a napkin!' thundered Gillian as she pleaded with her thirty-year-old-son to stop using a naan bread to wipe his face.

'Oh, keema!' Jason said after taking a bite, then resumed using it as a napkin.

I took that as a sign to slope off to the sofa, my bed for the night, it having been made up by Pamela hours before.

'Right next to Ritchie's,' she had told me with a wink. Got to appreciate the effort.

I did have a cuddle with Richie and fell asleep with him in fact. Fully dressed, of course. Although I don't actually remember falling asleep. We had all drunk a lot of the champagne meant for the 'New Year's Eve Extravaganza!' When I had asked Pam if she was sure it was okay to have the bottles with the sticky labels plastered over them that read ***If you drink this before the 31st you will ruin the whole of New Year's Eve***, she had replied,

'Of course, darling, let's live a little.' Probably will have a very different view of it in the morning though, once the Valium wears off and the hangover kicks in.

CHAPTER 16

31st December, Midwinter Lodge, Tomatin, The Scottish Highlands

I woke up early and extremely hungover, so sloped off for a bath and a cup of coffee before Chloe woke up. I started thinking about the text again as I sat in the kitchen window seat, looking out at the still-dark garden, little squeaks coming from the boot room. (Puppies, not mice, I hope.) I mean, Richie seems happy enough with me, when he's with me, maybe it is nothing? But then when people write or talk about their partners cheating, they always say, I thought he or she was happy until I found out they had been sleeping with my brother/ work colleague/slutbag called Nicole. *I've come back an hour later to add that I shouldn't really be calling Nicole a slutbag as I don't know who she is or what she knows. For all I know, it's innocent and they're just good friends, like Val and Adonis (hopefully not quite as good friends as those two, actually) or there is much more to it, but Nicole doesn't know anything.

At least nothing has really happened between us. Physically, anyway. But there is a lot to be said for an emotional connection, isn't there? Or have I been kidding myself about that as well? I really feel that we had a connection from the beginning. But maybe that's just what I want to believe. If Richie is also seeing women like Nicole, who looks as though she should be on a

Timotei advert, then I am actually thankful nothing more has progressed between us. I may have lost a lot of weight, but I am not beach ready. God, I am not even dark bedroom ready.

Pam and Gillian have booked a horse-riding trek booked later today. Will be good to clear my head. The brochure promises 'two hours of epic trails with panoramic views, whilst enjoying the peace and tranquillity of magical forestry'. I had been disappointed that the trekking stables advised against Chloe joining in due to 'extreme weather and terrain'. But Grandad has said he would take her and Jenna's boys to look for red squirrels and then toast marshmallows over one of the fires, so she's happy enough.

'Right, gang!' said Pam, who was much brighter after I had ushered her away for an extra-long shower and two aspirin while I had tackled last night's disaster zone left in the dining room. 'Today's agenda. Those of us taking part in pony trekking will leave at eleven and returning around three this afternoon. Nigel and Hilary arrived back this morning, after being postponed longer than expected. They have also asked me to mention that they are holding a sound bath session in the library after lunch, when they have recharged their, erm, batteries, should any of you like to take part.'

'Nah, fool me once, shame on you, fool me twice, shame on me,' said Maggie, shaking her head as she stabbed her fork into the last quarter of her American pancake, using it to mop up the last puddle of syrup on her plate. 'Besides, I've decided to tag along with you lot. I need some fresh air after all that booze last night.'

'Excellent!' said Pam, sounding genuinely pleased. 'I've just rustled up a delicious chicken casserole and baked potatoes for those of you staying behind. It will be in the Aga. Richie has offered kindly to dish and serve at one p.m., prompt. If any of you leave the house, please take the blue rucksack. It in contains first-aid kit, flares, life raft and thermal blanket. Nana has agreed to check Diana and the puppies, every hour on the hour and send me a text report, via Jenna's phone. Whilst Chloe, Maxwell and Roman go with Edward (my grandad), George, Barnaby and Jason to look at wildlife.

'Any questions?' Gillian asks.

Maggie raises her hand. 'Can you save me some of that chicken casserole, Richie, love? and a potato or two please, mate.' Pam tells Maggie she has prepared a hamper for us to eat in the car on the way home from our ride.

'Yeah, I know, Pam, mate, but that casserole will be a nice little snack just to keep me going til tea. What are we having again?'

'We are having our formal dinner if you remember, as part of our New Year's Eve extravaganza,' said Gillian.

'Yeah, I know, I'm lookin' forward to that. Got a sparkly number and three bottles of Archers in my case,' says Maggie. Nothing says formal black tie gathering like a sequin minidress from Oh Polly and a litre of Archers. Can't wait.

Richie had carried out my hat and coat, then opened the car door for me, leaning in to call a friendly 'drive safe' to Gillian, who was behind the wheel faffing about with her seat, and telling Pamela to help herself to the Murray mints in the glove compartment. Jenna looks away as Richie then leaned in further, wafts of Dior

Sauvage hitting my nose as he kisses me and murmurs into my ear that he would miss me.

The journey takes just under an hour; we chat mainly about the puppies, Jenna asking Pamela if she will re-home them all or keep one. Pamela makes uncommitted 'erm' noises admitting she may like to keep at least two, but wouldn't be making any decisions 'just yet.'

'Cor, it's like *Emmerdale* out there, ain't it?' Maggie marvelled as we took in the scenery.

'Well, I suppose, but *Emmerdale* is filmed in Yorkshire, and they have hills, but no mountains,' Gillian replies, with less sarcasm than usual.

'I've never been to Yorkshire, looks blindin', though,' Maggie says, while taking a video of the vast lake we're now passing from out of her window.

It's still drizzling when they finally find the turning for the trekking centre; the small handmade sign being almost completely camouflaged by thick ferns and stinging nettles.

'Well this isn't how it looked on the website,' said Pam as Gillian dithered about, trying to park the Land Rover in a small patch of the makeshift car park that's surface wasn't submerged puddles.

'Good grief, my poor Landie. It isn't built for such devastating terrain,' said Gillian as we all giggled and pointed out it, in fact, built for just that.

'I can't find no one called Nicole on his social media pages. I've even been on his old Bebo and Myspace account,' whispered Jenna to me as we made our way to the horse-trekking reception. (The caravan next to a skip.)

'I've asked Jase to sound him out while we're here, about his intentions and all that,' Jenna tells me as she pauses to bury her face in the neck of a chestnut gelding, tied up outside one of the stables. His coat is unclipped and wet.

'Cor, that smell it's universal, ain't it? That gorgeous, musky horse smell. Don't matter what horse you smell and where you smell it, it's the same smell. Bit like McDonalds, really. Big Mac in England or a Big Mac in Turkey. Still a Big Mac.'

Agreed with Jenna on both the horse smell and the Big Macs and then asked,

'I doubt Richie will tell Jason anything, will he? If he is seeing someone else?'

Jenna replied that, as she had already told me, men were dim, so Richie probably would tell Jason everything, and that Jason, although not a grass as a rule, is when she tells him to be, cos he's more scared of her than he is Richie. Which says a lot about Jenna, given Richie is six foot two, seventeen stone, and a trained fighter/killer.

'Jase knows where his bread's buttered, don't he? Fuckin' hell! Look at the size of that one! ' said Jenna, pointing at a large heavyweight cob being led out of a stable. Whose name turned out to be Wilbert and Maggie's mount.

I got paired with a dappled Connemara called Lady, Maggie was all smiles on Wilbert; she kept ruffling his mane and calling him a 'handsome big sod'. Gillian and Pam were beaming from ear to ear after being appointed matching Irish Sport horses called Summer and Autumn, who the manager assured me when I had raised concerns were 'docile schoolmasters'. Jenna had a very serious look on her face. She felt that her pony, Storm, who was the same size pony as Lynn, our riding instructor back at home, would place Chloe on, had sneezed twice and in doing so used it as an excuse to yank her forward 'passive aggressively and deliberately to shit her up'.

Jenna then got it into her head that Storm's name had a secret meaning, and kept asking the manager why he was called Storm, how many times someone had fallen off him and if he was a 'confirmed rearer.'

'He's had no more fallers off him than the rest of them, well, apart from Wilbert there who's like an armchair.'

Maggie's face had radiated upon hearing this, and started patting Wilbert and saying, 'You're a good boy, ain't ya? A gentle giant, good boy!' Just like a proud parent.

Jenna then said, 'What about the rearing? I need to know what I'm dealing with, mate.'

'Well he hasn't reared, to the best of my knowledge. You're not far from the floor anyway.' All very reassuring.

As we made our way through the forest; damp ferns swishing and brushing my feet as our group trotted through the small single file track, we all kept looking up into the sky, marvelling at the silver birch and various oaks and pines that seems to go on forever. Morale was high. As we passed through one clearing and were heading towards the next woodland, Jenna and I – at the back of the group – were chatting in low voices.

'What are you two whispering about? Maggie asked. I said nothing, but then Jenna said we may as well tell them and see what they think. I agreed, because when you're in a situation, especially one involving a man, you want opinions, and as many as possible.

'Etta has a problem,' Jenna announced, which got everyone's attention, especially Pamela's, who spun her torso around, holding onto the back of her saddle in one gloved hand, both reins in the other.

'Do tell, what is the problem?' Pam asked, her head and eyes darting between me, Gillian, Maggie and Jenna, then back to me, like a meerkat on crack.

'You know when Richie took Etta out for lunch the other day?' Everyone nods and Maggie says, 'Such a good boy, Richie, he knows how to treat a women.'

'Well, when Richie was buying drinks, Etta glanced, in totally a non-spying way, down at his phone on the table as a message came up, and it was from a picture of a girl wearing a bra and knickers.'

'It was more of a bikini,' I add as Jenna waves away my correction.

'Bikini, bra, same fing really, ain't it? So the bird had her tits out and the message said, sorry missed your call and that she could meet him on the 2nd of January,' said Jenna, eyes bulging in a 'what do you all think about that, then?' kind of way.

Pamela gasped and Gillian tutted and shook her head.

'That little bastard, you wait til I see him, he will be getting a bunch of fives from me! I knew he couldn't be trusted,' raged Maggie, changing her tune remarkably quickly.

'Let's not be the fools that rush in,' says Pam soothingly. 'It could be just a friend.' She was making a similar face that Jenna had pulled when she had said the same thing.

'Well, in that case, why, when Etta asked who it was that texted him, did he lie about it?' asked Jenna.

Gillian ducked from a low branch as we joined a downhill trail through more woodlands. I was expecting a cutting remark of some kind.

'From experience, if you think something's wrong, it usually is. I should know.' Jenna and I swapped looks.

Pamela urged her friend to: 'Not disclose anything she would regret', only for Gillian to reply she was sick of covering for 'That man who can't face his mistakes'.

Even Jenna felt sorry for Gillian by the time she sobbed her way through telling us that she wouldn't disclose details, but would say she had been 'to hell and back' in the last three months, and that she is still coming to terms with the 'staggering level of lies and deceit' that had come to light.

'You poor cow. I wouldn't have given you so much shit if I had known, Gill, mate,' said Maggie.

'You wasn't to know, Maggie. But I know I am amongst friends when I say that men, in general, 'are complete shits', sniffed Gillian as the tour leader called back that terrain would become more challenging and that we must keep two hands on the reins and stop leaning over to hug each other now.

It was actually quite a bonding experience, without sounding like a knob. Although following the tour leader's instructions and keeping our 'eyes facing front', we all chatted and took turn throwing ideas into the mix about what I should do about Richie.

Jenna had just suggested that we should all get together once a month, and that we should even have a weekend away soon, 'just us girlies', before getting told off for forgetting herself again and leaning over to squeeze Gillian's hand. Which, in itself, was quite a moment.

Then something unexpected happened. That's the thing about medical emergencies. They creep up on you when you least expect it; taking happy, high-spirited moments and plunging them into chaos and panic.

It all happened so fast.

That's what people always say, isn't it? But it's true. It did. A complete blur. One moment we were all giggling about Maggie's idea of a honey trap – a woman on *Loose Women* had employed one; she'd told us to see what her husband got up to on a work weekend – and the next we were waiting for an air ambulance.

'OH SHIT!' Jenna screamed as Pam's horse darted sideways, banging into Storm, Jenna's pony, and almost unseating her.

'Lean back, grab the mane!' shouted the trek leader, as Pam shot past her screeching, taking off like a bullet from a gun. My heart was pounding as I heard Pam's shrieked plea for us to 'DO SOMETHING!'

We all looked to the leader as Pam's horse threw two violent bucks in unison and Pam flew forward, somersaulting through the air. We all gasped as she landed awkwardly on her head, onto the rock-hard ground, before tumbling onto her back. But our trek leader doesn't know what to do any more than we do.

I've already dismounted and ran to Pam before the manager feebly instructs Maggie, Jenna and Gillian to 'dismount and stay put'. Maggie ignores the instruction, throwing her horse's reins in Gillian's direction and panting along behind me, as I run over to Pam.

'Pammy! Oh my christ, Pammy. Can you hear me?' Gillian calls as she joins Maggie and I by the side of Pam.

'Do NOT remove her hat!' Maggie shouted as she leaned down to Pam's side.

'You mustn't move, Pamela. You've taken quite a tumble. I'm going to get medical help. You must stay where you are.' Pam seems understandably dazed and confused, but mumbles a feeble 'right-o'. I hold her hand and tell her she is going to be fine. Hoping to God she will be.

It is then that we see a very different side of Maggie; none of us – apart from Jenna –knew that she volunteers as a St John Ambulance First Responder. With calm authority, Maggie instructs us all to take off our coats, remove and hand her our underlayer, then 'zip those coats back up, or you'll need an ambulance and all!'

We all watch on, Jenna and I sobbing now, as Maggie gets down on the wet ground – the slushy snow seeping into Maggie's pink jodhpurs – as she kneels down behind Pam's head.

'Pam, it's Maggie here, mate. Don't worry, I'm a first aider and I'm here to help ya. All above board and all that; I did all the courses, got my certificates and everything. On the wall in my lounge, they are. Have you noticed them before? I'm just gonna roll these jumpers up to put either side of ya head, mate, then I'm gonna hold ya head nice and still till the experts arrive, to protect ya neck.'

'Cindy,' says Maggie, calling over to the trek leader, who's standing silently, biting her nails. 'You got anything in that bag of yours to keep Pam warm?' Cindy seems a bit panicked and fumbles around until she pulls out and unwraps a silver blanket that you see marathon runners draped in as they pass the finish line, out of her saddlebag. Cindy holds it out to Maggie, who is still kneeling on the floor, with her elbows on the ground and her hands holding each side of Pam's head.

'Lay it over her, mate, I can't let go of her head.'

'I, erm, can't get a phone signal. I need to ride on so I can call for, umm, help,' Cindy stutters.

'Mum already sent my mother-in-law to phone 999, mate. Gillian done what you said, Mum,' Jenna tells Maggie now. 'And gave them our grid reference from her compass thing.' Jenna's face was etched in irritation at our so-called qualified guide's incompetence.

'Hear that, Pam? Gilly's been on the blower to 999 and has given 'em our location, so they will be here soon. Won't be long now.'

'It's just the shock, Etta, mate,' Maggie reassures me when I point out Pam's chattering teeth.

It's only when you think you're maybe going to lose someone that you realise how much they mean to you. I know that after today. I'm still shaking from the adrenaline. Everything went through my mind. Things I should have said and didn't, things I have said and wish I hadn't. The thought of having to tell my grandad and Chloe that the person who glues our family together isn't here anymore, because I had persuaded her to 'live a little' and come on the hack with us. This trek had been my idea. I had even promised her that 'nothing would happen'. Famous last words.

Horses are unpredictable, we all know that. A bit like people, in that they have their own minds and don't always make rational decisions.

It's probably only twenty minutes until they hear the delicious thundering hum of the air ambulance overhead. I've never heard a better sound. They land in the clearing and Jenna races to meet them.

'Oh dear, what's happened here, then?' asks the jolly paramedic as he dumps down his medical bag. I notice that his fleece smells of Lenor when he pauses asking me Pam's known medical history to give my forearm a reassuring squeeze. Maggie smiles proudly as the second paramedic tells her what a brilliant job she's done and takes over supporting Pam's neck.

'Hi, Pamela. I'm Ross, one of the paramedics. We're just going to put a neck brace on you, give you some pain relief, and then we will get you to hospital. We need to keep your back and neck still until we get you checked out as a precaution.'

Ross then tells Jenna the name of the hospital they will be taking her to, saying that we would need to follow by car.

As soon as the helicopter has taken off, we begin walking back to the centre, leading our horses. Jenna and Gillian had said they didn't want to ride again, not after what had just happened. The mood was sombre, our thoughts with Pamela. As if sensing our mood, the skies turned dark as our horses hooves clip-clopped back into yard, and we handed over our horses to the grooms, Maggie handing the three borrowed riding hats to Cindy. We all start power-walking to the car park, anxious to meet Pamela at the hospital.

'Erm, excuse me,' Cindy the trek guide calls to us, hanging over the rusty metal yard gate that's held up by a stack of bricks. 'Sorry to ask, but your friend paid for a two-hour ride and, well, you was out for actually nearly

three hours, so how would you like to pay the excess?'
We all looked at each other.

'The friend you are referring to is my best friend, who has just been flown away in an air ambulance, an air ambulance that only even arrived thanks to myself and my daughter-in-law with potentially severe injuries that would have been made worse because of you! The so-called guide didn't have a clue how to deal with the emergency! If my friend hadn't have been with us and been a skilful first aider and acted while you—' spat Gillian, stabbing an outraged finger in the guide's direction, 'stood there with your finger up your arse! Therefore, and I think I speak for everyone when I say this, you can go and fuck yourself! And if anything happens to my best friend and confidante, you, young lady, will be hearing from my solicitor who is ranked one-hundred-and-fifty-six in *The Legal 500*!'

'Couldn't have put it better myself!' I said as Jenna and I swap 'Did you just hear what I heard?' looks.

'I'll drive, mate. You're shaking,' says Maggie. Gillian hugs Maggie, thanks her and tells her she's 'an inspiration'.

I am inclined to agree.

CHAPTER 17

'Pamela Wilson, came in from ambulance?' I say urgently to the receptionist in A&E when we arrived at the hospital.

I watch the receptionist type, her long pink acrylic nails click click clicking on the keyboard.

'If you take a seat, someone will be with you soon.' The receptionist then gestures over to the waiting room, without looking up. Jenna and I take a seat next a coffee machine. It has a piece of paper with *Out of order* written in red marker pen Sellotaped across the front.

'I've rung your grandad, Etta, love, and Richie is going to run up to the main house and ask if he can borrow a motor and drive ya grandad here. They won't be long,' says Maggie, her voice quieter than usual. We all sit in silence then, waiting for news, Gillian crosses and uncrosses her legs and I watch a cleaner wheeling a bucket with a squeaky wheel as she works her way round the mushroom-coloured Polyflor, diligently placing and replacing the yellow warning sign as she goes. The cleaner has mopped over half the waiting room by the time a striking Indian woman in scrubs, pile of files and loose papers in her arm, appears from the swinging doors and pauses at the reception desk.

'You're the relatives of Mrs Wilson,' she said as she made her way towards us. I nod even though it was more of a statement than a question.

'Yes, we are. Is she alive?'

'Can she walk?' Jenna asks as she's sniffing into her tissue.

'Can we see her?' I add. The poor doctor doesn't know who, or what to answer first, as our words reach her in an urgent jumble.

The kindly doctor raises her palm and smiles. 'I'm Doctor Liner, one of the junior doctors here. Pamela is a little groggy from painkillers, and has been taken for a scan just to check all is well. As we understand it, she did have a fall, but she is awake and, how can I put it, alert and very interested in her care.' I bet she is, I think with a small laugh.

We follow Dr Liner back through the swinging door. The sign over head reads triage. We are shown to a curtained cubicle and told Pamela will be back shortly.

'Oh my christ!' gasped Jenna, pointing to the whiteboard above the empty bed space. 'Not only has she maybe broke her neck, she can't talk no more neither!'

Dr Liner kindly explained that nil by my mouth actually meant someone was not being allowed food or drinks for medical reasons and not that they had lost the ability to speak. And that had actually referred to a previous patient, not Pam, who had already had two cups of tea and a Rich Tea biscuit. The board just hadn't been updated yet.

I send Richie a Whatsapp asking him to tell my grandad what the doctor had said and not to worry. That Pam had had a biscuit and a cup of tea, knowing he would take that as a sign all was well. He sends back a thumbs up and a heart. I don't reply as I spot a bed being wheeled my way.

'Oh, here she is! Pammy, darling? Are you okay?' Gillian asks, rushing to the side of the bed still being wheeled into place by a porter with a Jessica Rabbit tattoo on his neck. Before much more can be said, another doctor, who, judging by his age and his bedside manner, is much more senior, strides over.

'Right, I'll take a quick look at your scan and X-ray, but I'm confident you just have a sprained arm and a bruised ego, Mrs Wilson.'

'I still have chest pains. I think I'm having a heart attack. I couldn't breathe,' replied Pamela.

'I suspect you could breathe, Mrs Wilson, or you would in fact by now be dead. Panic attacks and winding, which are common after a fall, are rarely dangerous. Back soon! he says as he strides back off in the direction he came from.

'Well that's good news!' I said, smiling at Pam.

'I wouldn't get ahead of yourself, Henrietta, darling, I know when I am dying, and I tell you, I'm in the midst of a heart attack here.' Jenna sucks in her lips, trying not to laugh, and Maggie encourages Pamela to ask for some gas and air.

'Take it while it's on offer, mate. I had it when I had Jenna. Oh, and actually, you should also ask for some of that pethidine as well. Best night of my life that was, when I had Jenna, well till it come to getting her out. 9 lbs 11oz, she was. Like getting a melon through a keyhole.'

'I *knew* it! Look!' Pam said, wincing as she points over to the desk area, where several nurses sat on the phone or writing notes. At the other side is a higher desk; a man stands holding a motorbike helmet and a red box.

'I *knew* it! I have internal bleeding! Or organ failure, probably both. They were just trying to keep me calm while they had emergency couriers bike me in replacements!'

'She's right,' said Jenna, looking worried again. 'I've seen that on *999: What's your emergency?* They do that all the time after road crashes and that.' Gillian agrees she has 'caught glimpses of the programme herself', and can confirm this to be true.

'How much money do you all have?' Pamela asks, her eyes still fixed on the man on the bike. Her eyes widen as the stern doctor accepts the box, catches our eyes and seems to look a bit awkward then walks off briskly with his head down. Gillian and I both say we didn't bring our purses, and Gillian had used the change in the car for parking. Jenna has her debit card, but is overdrawn. Maggie says, 'Hang on!' and digs round her bra, then pulls out her 'emergency fiver'.

'Ah! I also have an emergency ten-pound note in my phone case,' I offer.

I ask Pam what she needs money for. She said she's going to fold it up and pass it over to the doctor in charge before they take her down for emergency surgery.

'That might be nothing to do with you, Pammy,' Gillian said.

I agree and tell her that doctors have lots of patients, and that I doubted it was for her.

Maggie then said that we needed to prepare for the worst, as the doctor did look 'very shifty'. Pamela and Maggie start clinging onto each other then, with Pam sobbing.

'It's for me, I know it. I just know it. You need to slip the notes to the doctor when he comes back; you're the only one I can trust to do it,' Pam told Maggie. Charming, I thought. 'Just tell him to do all he can for me, darling. And,' says Pam, turning to me, 'If I don't make it, Etta, you can have my jewellery, the dogs, and my new air fryer.'

We all clock the doctor return the now-empty box to the man with the bike helmet. Jenna shoots me a 'oh bugger' face as he then heads our way.

'Here we go. He will probably rush me down to surgery now. I want you to go back to the lodge and enjoy yourselves. Have the party. I will be there in spirit, oh, and I want to be cremated and kept on the fireplace,' Pam says solemnly, taking a breath to compose herself.

'It's okay, doctor. You don't need to tell me, *I know*. I just need to phone my husband before you take me down,' Pam said through sobs.

'Let me shake your hand, doc, from one medical professional to another,' Maggie says, darting forward.

The doctor took great offence to Maggie's attempt at drop swap-style bribe. But then I explained that Pamela had seen the organ and blood transfusion delivery and that we were incredibly sorry for trying to bribe him with fifteen pounds in crumpled notes, but Maggie was just trying to ensure Pam got the best possible chance of life. The doctor's mouth started twitching as he called in several other members of staff, then told me to repeat my story to them. They all laughed then for a very long time.

Pamela looked more put out than relieved, when the doctor who was still doubled up in laughter wheezed, 'The man on the motorbike wasn't delivering organs, Mrs Wilson. I am very short-staffed here, so some days I do a bit of bribery of my own; I order takeaways so my colleagues stay late and help out. Today is one of those days. The man you saw is the delivery driver for the Tiger Balti.'

My grandad arrived ashen with worry despite my assurances while he was en route that Pam was fine.

'You gave me a scare!' said Grandad, clasping Pam's hand in his. None of us mentioned the organ mix-up. As Jenna had said, 'friends don't snitch on friends.' (Unless you're Jason and Jenna tells you to.) And mistaking a takeaway box for an organ transport vessel was an easy mistake to make.

CHAPTER 18

Richie drove Jenna and I home in the borrowed Defender while Pamela, who had decided it would be easier for her to get inside Gillian's Land Rover (Although I think Gillian's car not smelling of wet dog was also a strong contributing factor) and Maggie had also gone to keep an eye on Pam's 'vital obs'. Richie had made conversation all the way back: 'Did we have a nice ride until the accident?' 'Must have been scary' etc. and then telling us that the kids had been fine, but that Maxwell had been sick 'just a tiny bit' after eating a family bag of toasted marshmallows, sandwiched between half a packet of chocolate digestives to himself.

The snow had really started to fall again by the time we pulled into the driveway to the lodge. The glow from the fires in the dining room and sitting rooms steaming up the original windows, and the smoke escaping from the multiple chimneys, and the stresses of the day, made the lodge look so inviting.

'Like Downton Abbey, ain't it?' said Jenna.

We all piled in, breathing a sigh of relief to be home safe and sound. Gillian whacked on the Michael Bublé while I helped Grandad position Pam by the fire, an avalanche of pillows behind her.

Jenna's nana, upon hearing Pam was injured, had headed straight into the kitchen to rustle up some sausage rolls and cheese straws for a 'little snackie snack' to see us all through to dinner. While Maggie had sent Jason upstairs to fetch 'our wounded soldier' who'd been 'in the wars'. A pair of her fluffy socks, 'any fluffy pair still with tags on'. 'Ah, actually, Jase, mate, best make it either ones where the penguin's playing the piano or cats in sunglasses, but not the unicorns eating cake, it might be too triggering.' Called Maggie up the stairs after considering her previous instructions.

'Where is she? Where is my step-mother?' called my mum as she dramatically rushed towards Pam and collapsed in her lap.

'I've rung Nige and he's in the woods, sending you healing. He's on his way back now.' She sobbed. 'I've been beside myself.' Which was a bit strange as generally she only usually worries about herself.

'Best to grasp the nettle.' Gillian says as she sidles up to me while watching Richie bring a basket of logs from the stack into the great hall an hour or so later. 'The longer the wait, the worse the sting.' Jason hadn't found anything out, or, if he had, he wasn't telling Jenna.

'I told him, I find out you knew about this, you're goin' down with him!' Jenna told me as we talked in hushed tones.

I take a deep breath when he's placed the last log and dusts himself off and ask if I can have a word in private. Richie looks at me quizzically, but gestures for me to follow him into the smaller sitting room. As I sink down into the tall-backed flora-print chair, he clicks shut the heavy oak door.

'What's up?' Richie asks causally, sitting down on the sofa opposite my chair.

'Without sounding like a mentalist, you know when we was at the pub, and you said you had a text from work, who was it from?' I ask him, making a note to watch his body language. Gillian said she knew Barnaby was lying to her when she confronted him. Too much neck and ear rubbing.

'What are you on about? It was from work, like I told you at the time?' No emotion whatsoever. No giveaway signs. Umm.

'You work with women in their underwear then, do you?' I ask, bristling. That gets a reaction.

'What?' Richie asks sharply.

'I saw a photo of a women in her bra (well bikini, but same thing really, as Jenna pointed out earlier) come up in your messages. I didn't mean to look, it just flashed up and caught my eye. So you do you work and meet up with lots of nearly naked women? Or just the one? I suppose you've got to keep your options open, we're nothing serious after all,' I reply, equally sharply. Oh looks like we're doing this then, I think, as I feel my blood boiling. Richie rolls his eyes at my inverted comma fingers, as I say 'nothing serious'.

He stares at me then for a few moments. 'Why are you bringing this up again now? I told you I didn't mean anything by saying it. In fact, do you know what? I don't need this shit and I don't have to justify myself to you!' Richie says, standing up to leave. Me, never one to be outdone, marches over to the door to beat him to it, turning as I open the door.

'And, actually, I think you'll find I am the one that doesn't need this shit.' Ha, put that in your pipe and smoke it, I think as I storm out of the door only to be yanked back by my bloody jumper sleeve that had got caught on the door handle. 'For fuck fucking sake!' I ranted to myself, trying and failing to unlatch the chunky knit that's well and truly entwined in the metal of the door latch. 'I don't need help!' I bark as Richie huffs and walks over to me.

'Good, because I wasn't offering any!' came the gruff reply as he marched past me.

I take my jumper off and slide out of it, leaving it hanging from the door handle like a deflated balloon entwined in overhead cables. I throw myself back down on the raspberry Chesterfield sofa for a good ten minutes after. Feeling the highlands chill, I wrap myself in one of the throws, only to discard it again almost immediately. It smells like Richie's aftershave.

What was the expression on Richie's face? Disappointment? I'm sure, but because I had caught him out or just in me, I wasn't sure.

Jenna knocks on the door and comes in with a mug, stepping over the jumper like it is the most normal thing in the world.

'Did he admit it?' she asks, joining me on the sofa and offering me a bright-red drink. 'Thought you might like one of these. 'The festive punch and kick.'

I feign a small laugh and accept it. I start to tell Jenna what was said and about my grand exit being ruined by the door handle.

'Typical, ain't it? Always happens when you're on one. I was rowing with Jase once and said, "That's it, pal, I'm leaving. Get a good look at me, mate, you'll never see me again!" Off I went, only to have to knock on the door ten seconds later when I realised I was in my slippers, had no car keys and had no bra on!' We're interrupted by a knock on the door. I let myself hope for a second it's Richie, returned to apologise.

'Just thought I would let you know that Richie has just gone to return the Defender, and, well, he also said thanks for having him. He, erm, had his rucksack and holdall with him. So I think he may have, sort of, left,' said Gillian.

I asked Jenna what I should do now. Jenna admitted she didn't 'have a fuckin' clue'.

'Shall I get my mum and Pam? She's on her feet now by the way, so that's some good news, ain't it?'

'Yes, I think we should see what they think?' Gillian offered. 'And I'll ask Jason as well. If he said anything to anyone, it will be him. You know what men are like. Thick as thieves,' added Gillian as Jenna shot me 'a told-you-so look'.

I go to say yes, but I can't hold back the tears and speak at the same time. So I just nod. It's always the way, I think to myself. If life is going to well and everything seems too good to be true, it's because it is. Still, it was nice to feel happy, even for a short time.

Maggie thunders in wearing her *Elf* onesie, offering to phone Richie to ask him, 'What the fuck he thinks he's playing at.' But I say to leave him to it.

'He's deffo gone, mate,' says Jenna, gently offering me another drink of punch. 'Jase just told me that Richie said he was heading back for work and was going to get an Uber to drop him at the nearest bus or train station.'

'Good luck with that round here. Just Eat don't even deliver, remember!' Maggie said as though she had just been reminded we had no running water.

I tell everyone that 'I'm fine' and will 'deal with it when I get home' because clearly he is guilty, and that's why he's left. No point causing a drama and ruining everyone else's time.

'I doubt he would get far, it's New Year's Eve,' said Pam. 'Shall I get Grandad to go after him? I would go myself, but this punch has quite a bit of punch and kick, and what with my dice with death this afternoon, I am a little shaken.' I thank Pam, but say no thank you, but that I appreciate her. And I do.

I can see everyone looking at me with pity, so I decide to say something.

'It's New Year's Eve and we're all healthy and together, well apart from Richie, but that's his choice. Nothing will get resolved with him and I at this moment in time. If there even is a him and I at this point, so let's just all have a nice evening. It's the least we can do after all the effort Pamela and Gillian have made for us all. Agreed? I ask the room.

'Yeah, Etta, mate, I agree. Actually, there is something Mum and me wanted to ask,' says Maggie. 'Why us two take over the cooking for tonight? Give you both an evening off?' Maggie asks Gillian and Pam. I wait for the barrage of excuses.

'That sounds perfect, doesn't it, Pammy? Thank you, Maggie. That's *so* very kind of you,' says Gillian.

'It really does,' Pam agrees.

'Well, I Pam Understand, cos she did hit that floor pretty hard. But Gillian? What's all that about? It's like she's had a personality transplant. Did you hear her swearing as well?' Jenna said.

Nigel swanned into the hall, Pam and Gillian looking up from a crossword, Jenna and I the other side, taking it in turns to play a driving game with the kids on their Nintendo DS.

Well, I had noticed that Nigel's skin had a tinge of orange about it, the last time I had seen him, but had thought little of it; put it down to all the carrot juice he slurps or whatever. But when Jenna clapped eyes on him as he shook off his animal hind jacket, her face lit up.

'Ha! Caught orange-bloody-handed!' she said at the top of her lungs, turning over his palms and holding them up to the room. 'This man! This so-called psychic has been stealing my bloody face cream!'

Nigel really was a shocking shade of tangerine. Nigel, however, had the audacity to claim he didn't have the first idea 'of what you're accusing me of, man!'

Mum, never far from drama, skipped in then, standing in front of Nigel, her arms out sideways in a protective stance, and wasted no time in shouting that Jenna should 'get her facts right' and that her husband 'Only ever used ethical and fully vegan brands!'

Maggie came bustling in then, asking, 'What's going on here, then?' while puffing out her chest in my mum's direction. Mum looked a bit scared then and asked if Maggie could kindly ask her daughter to 'stop making false accusations against her husband'. And that they could in fact 'Start a claim against Jenna for slander and defamation of character' as Nigel 'would rather die than use animal products'.

'Well he obviously is full of shit cos he's been using my bloody Estée Lauder face cream that I laced with tanning drops!' Raged Jenna.

Mum got all shouty then, but hid behind Nigel and said she 'demanded proof!'

'Proof?' laughed Maggie. 'Look at his fuckin' face! He's like a fuckin' Oompa Loompa!'

'You're a liar, mate. I knew someone had been nickin' it, so I put tanning drops in it to catch the thief out! And last night I put ten drops in. Look at his face! I bet he had a shower or bath in the main bathroom when you got back today, didn't he?' Jenna retorted to my mum, getting just as shouty.

Jenna's nana comes in to see what all the noise is about.

'What's this in aid of, then?' Nana asks, glancing over at Nigel. 'Blimey, what happened to you, Nige, mate? You look like you've been somewhere proper hot!'

'Yes, like the sun,' adds Gillian dryly.

Jenna again explains that she planted a trap with self-tan tanning drops and now Nigel is orange.

Gillian tutted and asked Nigel what he 'had to say for himself' and Nigel replied, 'I will not get into negative energy-swapping with you soul-drainers.'

Pam suggests that Nige pays to replace Jenna's face cream and that be an end to it.

'We will do no such thing! For one we do not have any money, we're traders. We swap our skills for things we need! And, for two, like I have already just said, Nigel doesn't use non-vegan products!' Mum shouts again, clearly feeling much braver now there is a sofa between her and Maggie.

Nigel isn't as lucky as he is in collar grabbing distance to Maggie, who does just that. Tugging him into her and demanding him to 'tell the truth, ya little shit!' It seems Nigel, who fearlessly fights off demons and evil spirits, isn't so brave when it comes to a very agitated Maggie screaming, 'Tell the truth! You don't fool me! I Googled dog pregnancy, I knew somethink weren't right. Sixty-three days! You didn't have anything to do with that! You are as fake as Gilly's tits! No offence, Gillian.'

'None taken!' Gillian replied, a broad smile spreading across her face.

'It was a moment of weakness! Sorry, sweetheart. It's the weather. My skin was so dry, so itchy,' Nigel howls, falling to the floor dramatically as Maggie releases her grip.

'How could you!' Mum screamed in response and stropped out of the room.

Jenna is still pouting at Nigel, arms folded, as she refuses my grandad's offer of reimbursement, when my mum flounces back in, carrying a huge joint of cooked ham in both hands.

'I've brushed my teeth with charcoal, and not the posh stuff the people from Love Island use, no, actual FUCKING charcoal, I have bathed in freezing cold bastarding steams to re-align my chakra, I've eaten fucking nothing but seeds and sodding beetroot, while *you*, YOU, are using non-vegan face cream! Because your skin is dry! Well look at my pissing hair! Grey! It's grey and can I use Nice and Easy? NOOOO, because it's not fucking vegan, but you can use face cream! Is your need greater than mine? NO IT'S NOT! Well, *FUCK YOU*! And with that she swings the ham joint around, bashing Nigel round the head with it, then raises it to her mouth, bites off a massive chunk and starts chewing, while making exaggerated 'yummm-ummm' noises and screaming, 'Lovely fleshy pig non-vegan flesh, ummmmm delicious!' While we all stand looking at her, speechless.

So this is what losing your shit really looks like, I think.

'Yummy fucking ham!' Mum shouts, gnawing away at the meat joint as Maggie tries to guide her out.

'Come on, Hilary, mate, let's get you some mustard and a nice soft bap to go with that,' giving Nigel, who's being sick into the decorative coal scuttle from the fireplace, the evil eye and an 'I'm watching you' gesture with her index and middle fingers as she passes.

CHAPTER 19

A bath, bottle of wine and a family bar of Dairy Milk later, my mum joined Gillian, me, Jenna, Maggie, Nana and Pam in the main sitting room.

'That's the thing with men. You think you can trust them, but you can't, not fully. Not even the one's with large pensions,' Gillian sighs.

'Some men, not all, darling,' corrects Pam, uncovering her legs from a woven shawl.

'That's true, there are the odd rare gem. Like Edward. You are very lucky though, Pammy, darling,' agrees Gillian.

'The thing is,' says my mum. 'I couldn't give a toss if Nigel is vegan, or a meat eater or a healer. But the fact that he pressures me to live a certain way, questioning my moral compass, and then it turns out that he hasn't even living by the rules he imposes on others!'

'Do you really believe all that healing psychic stuff?' Jenna asks my mum kindly.

'Do I hell! He's a phoney, but I was caught under his spell. No more! There's no going back from here. They say money is the route to all evil, but they're wrong, it's men. Men are the route of all evil.' Mum sobs.

'But I'll be alright. I will come and stay with you and my dad, Pam. Help you with the dogs and spend time with my little girl,' she says, taking my hand. I don't know who's looking more alarmed at this point, me or Pam. Feeling a bit panicked at the thought of my mum moving into Pam and Grandad's, I divert the conversation and ask if it's time to get dressed for dinner.

'Gilly and I have said we are scrapping the black tie and for everyone to just wear what they feel comfortable in, darling. We're all amongst friends, after all' said Pam.

After a long, oily soak in the roll-top bath, I moisturise and towel-dry my hair, scrunching it with curl cream to keep the frizz at bay. On Pam's assurance that I could wear anything comfortable, I slip into my red tartan flannel PJs and matching slippers that Yana had got me for my birthday.

It seems I had the same idea as everyone else, as, when I re-joined the group everyone from Chloe, who had her new pony PJs on, to Gillian and Pam, who had changed into matching peach velour lounge sets. Even Maggie, who appeared to announce that 'grub was up' did so in a cosy onesie and flamingo slipper socks.

The only person that didn't get the comfortable clothes memo was Jason, who burst through the dining room door just as we had got seated wearing a sharp black suit and dickie bow-tie.

'Evening, the name's Bond. Jason Bond. Licence to thrill 007,' he shouted in a posh accent.

'Double 0 dickhead, more like!' Gillian, who'd had quite a few glasses of Maggie's Kick and Punch punch, shouted back as we all dissolved into laughter.

'Do you know what Gilly, mate? I used to think you was a knob. Like a complete and utter tosser, but you're actually alright, like really alright,' Maggie told Gillian as she walked around the table offering Bisto gravy from a plastic jug to each of us.

'Lovely bit of sausage and mash. Can't beat it, can ya,' Jenna's nana declared as we all tucked in.

'You really can't,' said Mum, who had asked to swap seats with Barnaby so she could sit next to me. 'I'd love another sausage if there's any going? What about you, Etta, would you like another sausage?' said mum, squeezing my hand. I said no thank you, but squeezed hers back. All very weird.

'Is Nigel in your room?' I asked quietly. Mum said no; he had been collected by his friend Clementine who he'd met via her advert on Gumtree about the life regression therapy hut she ran a few towns away.

'Probably for the best,' I replied. My mum nodded and wiped away a single tear that was making its way down her cheek.

'Yes, probably for the best. Are you sure you don't want any of these sausages? I want to eat them all, but I ate an awful lot of ham earlier. My eyes are bigger than my belly.'

I realise I am not that dissimilar to my mum, not really. Yes, she is quite a bit more selfish than I am, and she has a tendency to be awfully bitter, but then who am I to judge? Life wears you down after all. She's been me, but I've yet to be her.

That in itself deserves some compassion and respect. I decide in that moment to try to be a daughter and to let her try to be my mother.

We had all been waiting to open our presents to each other until this evening, so, after Barnaby and my grandad had loaded the dishwasher and Jenna and I had cleaned the dining room table and packed the place settings away, we congregated back in the sitting room. The snow, that's still falling heavily, settling into piles, mini avalanches on the window seals outside. It reminds me of the year Pam discovered snow in a can and went around blurring the bottom of the windows.

'Right, now the children have had their gifts. Shall we start ours?' asked Gillian.

My grandad went first and seemed chuffed with his *Gardener's World* subscription and said how brilliant and thoughtful Richie's gift, a backgammon board, was as he read the tag out loud. 'You mentioned before you used to play, so I thought we could have a few games.' Looks like that's out the window.

'Here you are, darling, this is from me and your grandfather,' Pam said proudly, handing over a wrapped shoebox-size present. 'I can't take the credit for this one!' Pam tells the room. This was all your grandfather's idea and he wrapped it, well, he wrote the tag, I wrapped it,' Pam continued, leaning into Maggie. 'You know how men can be with Sellotape.'

I was a bit confused when I opened the box and saw what was later explained to me as a tool to break a window if you have a car crash and need to escape. I said thanks as enthusiastically as possible.

'There is some more in there, darling!' Pam prompted, so I had another look and pulled out an envelope. Inside was a paid invoice for an intensive course of driving lessons.

'We thought that as you and Richie are courting and him living in *Wales*, it would be good for you to be able to drive,' Grandad explained. Ignoring Pam's frantic cut-throat gesture, I hugged and thanked them both.

'Which brings me onto my present to you!' Pamela announced, clapping her hands together and leaning down to present Grandad with a smaller wrapped present. He looks utterly perplexed as he pulls out a toy Range Rover.

'I think I've got the wrong gift,' Grandad says, offering it back to Pam.

'No you haven't! It's a Landie! I've bought you a LANDIE! Just like Barnaby and Gillian's! Isn't that marvellous, darling? It's being made in the English-based factory as we speak!' Grandad doesn't look that thrilled, probably because he is thinking how much his present has just cost him. But he then cheered up a bit when Pam pointed out that I would soon need a car, now that I was 'going to be a driver'.

'We can't have our granddaughter and great-granddaughter driving around in a used car with uncertain history, can we, darling? At least this way Etta can have our Picasso, and you know it's been serviced every ten thousand miles with a certified dealer. You can't put a price on safety.'

My mum apologised, and said that she hadn't got any presents for anyone as 'Nigel the knob' didn't believe in Christian holidays, but she would get everyone something in the sales.

We all had a little break from presents then, as the four casserole dishes of apple crumble were ready. To be honest, I was considering taking Pam back to the hospital and demanding another brain scan after she told everyone to 'grab a bowl and come and get comfy on the sofa'.

Gillian helped Pam go and check on the pups, while Jason set up the drone Chloe had got for Christmas from Maggie, Jenna and family.

'Thirty quid off amazon. Bargain, they are. The boys loved theirs, shame it broke when it crashed into Jenna's next door's greenhouse really. Right old fuss they made. Their own fault, though, who has a greenhouse next door to a house with two young lads?' Maggie told us, shaking her head.

I went with Jenna to stand under the shelter of the front porch, as she stood outside smoking, like she always does after food. We had tried to call Yana, Nicky and Val and had got no answer. And were just wondering why none of them had texted back since this morning.

'Matt promised he was leaving this morning, didn't he?' I asked. Jenna said he had, but that he had said it so many times, she wasn't holding her breath.

'They are probably busy helping Nicky; either getting them out of the house, or cleaning the house because they have left. It was in a right state Val said the other da— What the!' says Jenna, nudging me and nodding towards the entrance gates. It takes my eyes a few moments to adjust, with the snow and the outside lights causing bad visibility and a glare.

'There's someone coming up the drive,' I said to Jenna.

'I know! Let's get in quick. This is how horror movies start, this is. It could be anyone,' Jenna replied, throwing the rest of her cigarette into the snow.

CHAPTER 20

'Jase!' There's someone coming up the drive! Jenna calls as we close the front door. My heart leaps from my chest as we crowd together, looking out of the dining room window. I momentarily think and hope it's Richie. Then I clock the posture, and the Aztec coat.

It's not Richie. It's Nigel. I feel the flood of anticipation merge into disappointment.

'My friend's van broke down, can you someone give us a tow?' asked Nigel in the tone someone doing someone else a favour.

'I thought you would rather walk a thousand miles than step into my fuel-guzzling pollution magnet, old son?' Barnaby asked while reaching for his coat.

My mum, who must have been told Nigel was back, or perhaps heard his voice, shot out of the sitting room into the hall.

'It's too late, Nige. We are simply not the twin souls that you led me to believe. There's nothing you can say to make me change my mind,' said Mum like she was letting down a teen crush.

Nigel rolled back his coat sleeve and ripped off his hair wedding bracelet with his teeth. 'You are preaching to the choir. I have already informed the high priestess of Bethnal Green that I invoke my right to void the marriage she witnessed between us.' Mum was still sniggering and repeating, 'What was I thinking? He has the arms of an eight-year-old boy.' under her breath, long after Nigel had followed Barnaby to the Land Rover and Gillian had called after them 'Make sure he sits on the dog throw!'

'Good riddance to him!' Grandad said supportively, when mum's laughter started to verge a bit of the manic side. 'Don't worry, love, you can stay with us til you get on your feet. I'll have a word with Rodger; his son's the manager at Toolstation now, see if we can't get you a nice little job.' I expected Mum to start crying then. Because I would have done if I was her. But she didn't.

'Thanks, Dad, I'd appreciate that,' said mum.

Jenna and I take the kids up for a bubble bath and settle them down in bed. It must be the fresh air, as when I check on them half an hour later all three of them are sound asleep.

Back down in the sitting room, a re-run of *Only Fools and Horses* is playing in the background. Jenna asks if we should open the rest of the presents.

'Just waiting for Barnaby to get back,' Grandad tells her.

'Ah, there he is, finally. I was starting to worry that he'd got lost! Easy done in these conditions,' says Maggie's husband, George, half way through another episode. One of my favourites, actually. *Play it cool, Rodney, play it cool.*

'Everything okay, darling?' Pam asks Barnaby as he comes in and heads straight to the fire, rubbing his hands.

'Yep, all sorted, the weirdo is on his way,' Barnaby confirms.

'Although I did pick up another straggler on my way back,' Barnaby adds.

Jenna and I swap puzzled locks at this. My hopes are confirmed as Richie, whose Kristofer Hivju vibes are stronger than ever, with flecks of snow in his beard and flame hair that's tied up in a man bun, appears at the door. His frame seems even more towering than usual as he fills the sitting room doorway, offering a small smile to everyone who greets him.

'No work after all? You've been gone hours, do you want some food? There's plenty of sausages left, darling, shall I make you a nice sandwich?' asks Pam, warmly.

'Thanks for the board, Richie. Lovely job, that is. Thanks. Fancy a game later?' Grandad says, radiating genuine enthusiasm.

'Thanks, Pam, but you rest. I can grab something in a bit, and a game sounds like a plan!' Richie says brightly. 'And indeed, no work after all.' Richie then said that he had got to the train station and changed his mind, then couldn't get a taxi and that his phone had 'run out juice' so he decided to walk back.

'I am just going to have a shower and get some fresh clothes on, but could I have a chat with you, Etta, first, though?' said Richie, smiling at me and gesturing past the door he is standing by. I try not to look at Gillian, Pam, Nana, Jenna or Maggie, who I know will all be gawping at me as I squeak, 'Yes, sure', stand up and slope out of the door.

CHAPTER 21

'Can we talk upstairs?' Richie asks me while leaning down to his backpack in the hallway, and pulling out a pair of tracksuit bottoms, some socks and a hoodie.

I nod, giving him what I hope is a haughty face, even though I'm thrilled he is back.

'You forgot boxers,' I said, sulkily.

'I don't wear boxers.' Well that shut me up.

Have you noticed how men seem to be much more comfortable with nudity and in their own skin than women? Maybe it's less social pressures on men; woman are conditioned to look pretty for them, when some of them don't even brush their teeth.

I don't know why it is, but they never seem as shy or embarrassed about nakedness as women. Or maybe they are, but they just hide it better.

He holds open the main bathroom door, locking it behind us.

'Nicole is someone I work with,' he tells me as I perch on the closed toilet seat. 'She takes the bookings, does the social media and Pilates,' Richie says, stripping off under the overhead spotlights. Completely comfortable in himself. See. Absolutely mindboggling.

'I was ringing her to ask her to cover for me, that's all. Nothing more,' he says, reaching in and turning the dial of the shower on.

'So stop thinking mental thoughts. Just because your ex was a tosser doesn't mean I am, okay? I admit when I was younger, yeah, I was also a tosser, but I'm not twenty-five anymore,' he calls out to me from under a powerful rain shower. I stare at a screw on the wall in front, feeling my cheeks flush.

'I'm sorry then,' I say, smirking at him. 'Jenna would go mad if she just saw how much of her shampoo you just used.' Because that's me all over. Feel nervous or uncomfortable – make a joke.

'Not joining me, then?' he asks as I pass him the towel he gestured to on the rack at the side of me. I can tell by his tone, light and playful, that he's joking, but only half joking.

'I'm not that kind of girl!' I say. Thinking, good god, what would I look like in this bright light and no covers to tug over my wobbly bits.

'Worth a try!' He says, pulling me into him for a kiss, the shower jets firing and then bouncing off of the glass wall and soaking me.

'You're practically in now anyway,' said Richie, his hands pulling me into him.

I am just debating my next move, the pros and cons, when the moment is lost to darkness.

CHAPTER 22

'Don't worry! It's a power cut! But we are equipped to deal with it,' Pam announced, advancing up the stairs with her coal miner's light strapped round her forehead. I couldn't help noticing she looked very nimble for someone that had claimed she wasn't sure if she wouldn't need 'rehabilitative therapy' just an hour previously.

'Here, take this, darling!' Cracking a glow stick and handing me it, clocking my damp top and hair and Richie standing with only a towel round his torso. 'Ooh soo-rree to interrupt!' she says, a knowing smile creeping over her mouth.

'Oh no we wasn't, we was just, erm,' I stutter.

'You don't need to explain, darling, we're all adults. I know the laws of the jungle. So glad you have made up.' Oh please don't wink. Oh yeah, there it is. The knowing wink.

'Although, once you are dressed, can I borrow you, Richie, darling? Gillian and I need a professional option. We were just discussing sending up a flare, you know, just in case things get bad?' Pam said, 'But absolutely no rush, whenever you're ready between now and the next ten minutes will be fine.'

We re-join the others in the sitting room, that is actually very cosy with candles burning on the fireplace. Jenna comments quietly, 'Fancy a wardrobe change and a little wash, did we?' as she clocks my new clothes and damp hair. My face colours further as I notice Pam nod at Gillian, for Gillian to then look over at me and then tap Maggie's arm, until they're all in a row giving me a double thumbs up.

'Take it they knew as well, then?' Richie asks, chuckling.

'Shall we finish the presents, then?' Maggie asks, knowing full well the only one remaining under the tree was my present to Richie, and his to me. 'Come on, Rich, give her the prezzie!'

Richie rolls his eyes at his auntie, but does as he is told, using his phone torch to illuminate the bottom of the tree and handing me a little box. And he takes a seat next to me on the sofa. Fucking hell, surely not, I think. It can't be, can it? I feel my heart pounding.

'Hope you like it,' he says. He's watching me, still on his feet, but not down on one knee.

It's probably a necklace, I think, smiling to myself as I take in the rag doll cat wrapping paper and the colour coordinated bow. I know from Maggie's, Jenna's and her nana's presents that they haven't help him. They all used the same Daffy Duck wrapping paper. 'Fifty metres for four quid!' Jenna had told me. Richie must have got the paper and bow himself specially for me, and it's touching.

I open the box and it's for an iPhone charger. For the second time I make a tit of myself, saying, 'Thank you, I love it!' And kissing him on the cheek.

'It's not a charger, mate,' says Jenna, shaking her head in an amused 'fucking hell' fashion at Richie, who is doing much the same and chuckling. I struggle with the box as it has been very well taped. After a minute or so Jase pulls out his keys and unfolds a multi-tool keyring and uses a nail file to slice open the box.

'What on earth do you think you are playing at, young man!' said Gillian, seeing the tool in his son's hand. You are a father and married man and you are carrying weapons? Did you take that to London with you on the 23rd for that job?' Jason confirmed that he did.

'Well you should be counting yourself extremely lucky that you wasn't stopped and searched! Especially with that tattoo on your arm! You'd have been arrested for knife crime!' Gillian said, nudging Barnaby to back her up. 'What do you make of your son taking weapons to his place of work in London?'

Barnaby shrugged and said that Jason was indeed 'A stupid little idiot'. Jason told them both to stop being so dramatic.

'Those Met police don't mess about, Jason. There was an article about a gentleman who got peppered and tasered after a misunderstanding about misplaced hand and a zip. But then the man was a *Guardian* reader, so who knows. Perhaps deserved,' said Grandad.

'En-nee-way!' sings Pam, who's by now as good as humming with anticipation 'What's in the box?'

I unroll a piece of paper. In neat, swirly writing is a note:

Dear Etta,

I have wanted to spend some time with you (Well, all of the time in fact) since we met and I also wanted to get you something nice for Christmas, that we could do together. So I thought it might be nice to go away for

a few day together, just us this time. And I remembered you telling me how you have always wanted to see the Lipizzaner Stallions in Vienna. So that's where we are going. Jenna's helped me book everything and I've also asked Pamela and your grandad to take care of Chloe. We leave on the 7th January and return late on the 10th.

I will make sure you have a lovely time. Merry Christmas. Richie. X

It even has an X.

I don't know if it's the Christmas spirit, or the warm fire and candlelit backdrop, or being so high up in the country? Maybe we aren't used to the altitude. But I feel myself tear up as I thank him. It seems to be catching as, before I know it, Pamela, Maggie and Jenna are also sobbing and smiling. Even Barnaby, George and Grandad take turns to shake Richie's hand and say things like, 'Well done!' And, 'Blinding idea that!' All the excitement nudges Jenna's nana, who fell asleep in the chair as soon as the television went off, to rouse from her slumber in confusion.

'What's all this fuss? What's all the blubbing about?' Nana asks, looking alarmed.

'Richie's taking Etta to Viennetta, Mum! They leave on the 7th January!' Maggie says. Maggie's mum narrows her eyes in Richie's direction. 'What's he taking her there for? You know how to show a girl a good time, don't you? Bloody ice cream factory! Although my neighbour went to Cadbury World in Birmingham and it had a half-price shop. You'll have to take a freezer box, mind.'

'No, Nana, Viennetta abroad, with the horses that dance,' Jenna said. Nana said she had never heard of that one.

'Shall we do our New Year hopes and resolutions?' Pam suggests. She gets us to do this every New Year's Eve. We have to write down on a piece of paper our wish or resolution for the new year, read it aloud, and then throw it into the fire.

Richie pulls me onto his lap as I consider what to write.

Jenna reads hers out loud first. 'My hope is to quit smoking. And my realistic one is to go back to St Lucia by next Christmas.' I see Jason grimace at this and have a little chuckle to myself when Jase reads his one next: 'Save money for the future.'

Grandad declares his is to 'do more for the environment'. We all laugh when Gillian says, 'That's easy, just lock Pam out of her Amazon account and that will save half a rainforest in packaging for a start.'

'Mine is to get a job,' Mum tells us between slugs of wine. Pam and Grandad both smile at her proudly. 'And to spend quality time with my daughter and granddaughter.'

Maggie nearly sets fire to her hair extensions as she leans into the fire to throw her piece of paper in. 'You're supposed to tell us what it is first!' Jenna says.

'Oh yeah. I did me and ya nana's in one go, cos she ain't got her glasses. Your nana's goal is to meet Danny Dyer, and mine is to lose eight stone, run a marathon, oh, and to also get a fast-tan-sun-bed.'

'Fair play,' said Jenna, nodding.

'What's yours, Richie, darling?' asked Pam. Richie said his was to work less and spend more time on the important things, like getting to know Chloe and spending as much time with me as possible.

I said mine was to do my access course and get accepted into university. I also added: 'spend time with Richie', but I didn't write that down in case his was something like eat more fruit.

Then Gilly and Pam said they would do theirs together.

'Well you've probably been wondering what our professional photo shoot was all about?' Pam asked, beaming at Gilly.

'Well! Actually, you tell them, Gilly, you're better at public speaking than me, darling.'

'Okay, although that's something you will have to work on! Given the circumstances.' They hahaha then while the rest of us swapped amused and puzzled glances.

'The reason for the photo shoot was because we are launching ourselves!' Gillian said.

'That's right, from January 3rd, we will be lifestyle gurus, giving fashion, cooking and life advice on Instagram and possibly YouTube, if we can ever find that confirm your account email!' Pam enthused.

'We will be taking sponsored posts, hosting Instagram live chats and posting daily tips!' said Gillian, then eyeing us both keenly to gauge our reactions.

'Sounds fuckin' brilliant!' Maggie says. 'Let's have a little toast to you, shall we?' We all raise our glasses.

'Before we do, could I just say a few words?' asks Barnaby, getting to his feet. I hear Nana whisper to Jenna, 'Which one's he again?' And Jenna confirms that he is Barnaby, her father-in-law, Gillian's husband and Jason's dad.

'I knew his face, I just couldn't place him,' said Nana.

'I would just like to say a few words about my resolution for the new year,' he stutters, walking over to Gillian, clasping her hand and turning to face her.

'I know I've made mistakes, unforgivable mistakes, and with the lies I have told, I am lucky that you have agreed to give me a second chance. So my promise to you, Gillian, is that I will spend all of this new year making it up to you, and to show my commitment I would like to present you with this.'

Barnaby then gets down on one knee and presents Gillian with Ocado and Waitrose gift cards.

I hear Jason ask Jenna, 'Have I missed something?'

'Never again, Gillian, I promise. Never again.' Gillian accepts the cards and says,

'Apology accepted.'

Everyone is completely flabbergasted. Since when did a few hundred quids' worth of vouchers buy you out of, as Gillian referred to it, 'unforgivable betrayal and a mind-blowing level of deceit'.

'Well, I think you're repulsive! What you did to my poor Gilly, you're lucky you ain't my fella, cos I think all cheaters should have their knobs cut off!' Maggie said. Barnaby looked a little taken aback, but said he 'agreed wholeheartedly'. Gillian looked all grateful and mouthed 'thank you' at Maggie.

I changed the subject, and asked Maggie's husband, George, what his resolution was.

'I'm thinking about getting back into playing the guitar,' he said, his voice polite and softly spoken as ever.

'Nigel, my…' I can see Mum pause, considering what to call him: 'Ex, left his guitar here, should I fetch it? Maybe you could play us something? As the power's still off? Bit of music to see in the new year?' Mum suggested.

George seemed very keen on this idea. Noticing that it was now only twenty minutes until midnight, I went with Pam, Jenna and Maggie to get some more bottles of champagne and clean glasses.

'Come on, Pam, I am dying to know! Who was it Barnaby was having it off with? His PA or the cleaner?' asks Maggie while sidling up, holding up her hand to cover her face like she was conspiring to kill someone.

'I really couldn't say,' Pam said, shaking her head. Pam then takes a further one minute of colluding to break and tells us that Gillian, who had 'great suspicions' that 'games were afoot' when Barnaby had started offering to do the weekly grocery shopping and put it away, whilst Gillian was at Fit After Fifty with Pam. And so Gillian had ordered a batch lot of nanny cams off of Amazon, and had a workman come and set them up in all the rooms. Apart from the toilets, as that would have been a 'step too far.'

'You should have seen him, walking in bold as brass he was with *Aldi* bags! Neither of us could believe it. Poor Gillian was sick with rage by the time we had watched him scrape out the replica Lurpak from its container and tipped it into their empty genuine packaging. And it didn't end there! Cornflakes, Fairy, orange juice. Gillian kept saying after, 'I know it's my husband on the screen, but I just do not want to believe it is him.' Shook her to the core. We confronted him and he was overwhelmed by the evidence; he came clean and admitted it, and that he had been doing it for weeks! Said that he had been influenced by the credit card bill, and Aldi's admittedly very aggressive advertising' Pam whispered sensationally.

'Sorry, so let me get this right. All those bloody pats on that back I gave Gill when she was sobbing about 'lying, deceitful men' was because she caught Barnaby replacing Aldi cornflakes into a box of Kelloggs?' demanded Maggie

'Well, no, there was a lot more to it than that, darling,'

'Ahh, So he was shagging someone! Was it the store manager? I've seen her in there a few times. Thinks she's better than the rest of his with her lip-filler and Lewie Wee-tonn shoes. Wouldn't give me my refund on that paddling pool. You remember Jen? She said it weren't designed for adults. Rude as they come, her!'

'There was no lovemaking, but there was emotional cheating. You know how Gillian feels about budget supermarkets. It was a violation of her trust!' said Pamela

'If he can lie about that, he can lie about anything, I suppose,' said Jenna.

'He's deffo shaggin'' the store manager,' says Maggie to me and Jenna in a low tone. All that butter swapping. It was a metaphor.' Nodding at us slowly with a very self-assured look on her face.

'I'd just like to say a few words,' says Pam. 'Now I would like to thank you for coming and to apologise that our big New Year extravaganza has turned into a lot more of a low-key affair. But at least we are all together.'

'To being together!' Richie says, raising his bottle of Budweiser.

'To be straight with you, Pam, this is the best New Year I've had in years. Beautiful gaff, good company, plenty of Archers, and the love of my life about to give us a tune on the guitar. What's not to love!' We all agree. I for one have had a New Year's I will always remember.

'Why don't we all let out the old and in with the new by the front door? It's nearly midnight and I'm dying for a fag,' Jenna's nana suggests.

We spent the last few minutes before midnight wrapping ourselves in coats and blankets and huddle by the front door. The sky is clear, and full of stars.

Jenna, who has left her mobile upstairs in the hallway, torch on, in case any of the kids woke up and is scared, jogs back in to retrieve my phone, that's still in the sitting room, face down, the torch function beaming. She manages to connect it to BBC iPlayer. We all embrace as we hear the familiar chimes of Big Ben. The sound of hope and fresh starts for so many people.

'Happy New year!' we all shout as Richie embraces me, pulling me into him.

'Etta, mate, I am sorry, but I need to show you something. It won't wait,' says Jenna, tapping me on the shoulder.

CHAPTER 23

'A notification reminder just came up, mate. It's from Val,' said Jenna, showing me my phone.

Val 11:23pm

Sorry to put a dampener on your break, ladies, we did hope not to bother you, but not only has Nicky's guest not moved out, but after today and us all finding out some very concerning information about them, it's clear this is going to need all our heads together. So can you please let us know when you're on your way home and an ETA? We need to all meet asap. Happy new year. Love Val. X

'That doesn't sound good,' I say, biting my lip.

'There's something else, And I don't know what the message said, as it came through on your Facebook Messenger notification as I unplugged the charger. I just saw the name. It said, *Nicole Harrison wants to send you a message.*

'She will just be explaining, what Richie already has,' I said, bringing up the request. The photo, this time of a girl with perfect white teeth standing against a bar, stares back at me. 'I don't need to read it,' I announced, declining the request.

'Okay, mate, if you're sure. Happy New Year!' Jenna says, swinging me round.

I snuggle into Richie's chest.

'What did Jenna want?' asks Richie as he wraps his arm around my waist, on the front steps of a hunting lodge in The Scottish Highlands; Pam and Gillian are sharing a bottle of Baileys, taking turns to swig it directly from the bottle, Grandad is chatting to Barnaby and my mum about the 'very competitive rates of pay' at Toolstation. George announces that his next number is dedicated to 'The love of my life, Maggie, who's munching on chocolate biscuits and playing candy crush on her phone with her mum.

Jason laughs and pulls Jenna into him for a kiss, while she makes sick noises at the sight of her mum, winking at her stepdad and sucking her fingers suggestively.

As Barnaby's acoustic rendition of Sophie Ellis Baxter's Groovejet ('If This Ain't Love'*)* rings out, the stars that light the deep-black sky reflect on the sheets of snow that have covered the grounds like a duvet. I consider my reply.

'Oh just wanted to show me a message from Val about our other friend,' I say as Richie wraps his arms tighter around me. I debate not even mentioning the deleted message, but decide from now on honesty is the best policy.

'I got a message as well, a request from Nicole.' Did I imagine his body stiffen slightly? Then relax when I added, 'I just deleted it. No point reading what you have already told me, is there?' I say brightly.

I will admit for a second I read something into his change in body language. But I won't make the same mistake again. How can you find your happy if you're constantly chasing after misery that doesn't always exist? I decide to trust him. Until I have a reason not to.

'I wonder what they have found out about Matt?' I asked Jenna when we had all gone back inside. The house's lights having been restored.

'I dread to think, mate, but whatever it is we'll deal with it together, just like we always do.'

And Jenna is right. We don't always know what life will throw at us, that we cannot control, but what we can control is the people we surround ourselves with. And that's what's really important. Real friends and family. Because when all's said and done, they're the ones that will reach in and pull you up to the surface, when you can no longer breathe, knowing this makes us confident enough to swim.

'To us,' Jenna said, lifting up a glass of tropical juice Jason had just fetched her from the kitchen.

'To us and whatever the year may bring.'

The End – until next time.

Printed in Great Britain
by Amazon